Lazar Engles (Engelstern)

OUR PARTISAN KINGDOM

From the Vilna Ghetto to the Bielski Family Camp

Lazar Engles (Engelstern)

OUR PARTISAN KINGDOM

From the Vilna Ghetto to the Bielski Family Camp

Translated from the Yiddish by David Engles

יד ושם
YAD VASHEM
THE WORLD HOLOCAUST REMEMBRANCE CENTER

THE INTERNATIONAL INSTITUTE FOR HOLOCAUST RESEARCH

Lazar Engelshtern
In getos un velder
Fun Vilne biz di Nalibaker vildenis

Academic Editor: Daniela Ozacky Stern
Language and Production Editor: Adina Mendelsohn

Unless otherwise indicated, all photos in this publication are courtesy of the Engles family.

P.O.B. 3477, Jerusalem 9103401, Israel
publications.marketing@yadvashem.org.il
First published in Yiddish by Hakibbutz Hameuchad, 1972

ISBN 978-965-308-703-3

Typesetting: Hava Salzman
Printed in Israel by Ayalon Printing

In loving memory of our parents,
Lazar Engles, Ruth Engles,
Jacob Malek, and Lenke Malek,
who survived the Holocaust and
became the victors, triumphing over
the destroyers by having
the courage and conviction to
continue to observe the traditions
of Judaism and to transmit them
to their descendants.

CONTENTS

MY FATHER, THE YIDDISHIST FROM VILNA

In 1972, just a few years after making *aliya* to Israel, my father Lazar Engles (Engelstern)[1] had the great pleasure and personal satisfaction of publishing two books in Yiddish: one written by my mother Ruth Leimenzon Engles—also a Holocaust survivor—and the other written by himself. Each book recounts the personal experiences of its author during the three-year period immediately after the Nazi occupation of Vilna (Vilnius), Lithuania, in June 1941. The first book, titled *Farshribn in a shayer* (Written in a Barn),[2] was the diary that my mother wrote in 1944 while hiding in a barn from the Nazis on a farm just a few kilometers outside of Vilna. My father had guarded her handwritten manuscript for many years after her death and eventually brought it to Israel in 1968, where he succeeded in publishing it. The

1 Lazar Engles's original last name was Engelstern (transliterated from Yiddish as Engelshtern). It was changed to Engles when the family became US citizens.

2 Ruth Leimenzon Engelshtern, *Farshribn in a shayer* (Yiddish) (Kibbutz Lohamei Hageta'ot: Ghetto Fighters' House, 1972).

second book, titled *In getos un velder* (In Ghettos and Forests), was the book that my father started writing in 1945 when he began to jot down recollections that were still fresh in his memory about the horrific ordeal he had somehow miraculously survived.[3]

My father considered the publication of these two books, as well as his autobiography[4] published in 1976, to be among his most important achievements. He had two reasons for this. First, like many other survivors, he felt that he had a sacred duty to recount his experiences for future generations to remember. But he also had a more personal reason, which concerned me, his only son. He expressed this reason at the end of the short biography he wrote about my mother that appears in her book: "All these years, I have taken good care of the notebook, wanting to keep it with me until my son David was mature enough to be able to read it, and most important of all, to be able to understand what his mother had been through."[5] He often expressed this desire directly to me, not only about my mother's diary but also regarding the two books that he authored.

Fifty-two years after the publication of my parents' two Yiddish books, I now also have the great pleasure and personal satisfaction of publishing my English translations of these two books. My mother's book was published by Yad Vashem in August 2023 with the title *Written in a Barn: The Diary of a Young Woman from Vilna*. And now, just a few months later, my father's book has been published by Yad Vashem too.

My father was leading a peaceful and happy life in Vilna when the Nazis invaded Lithuania on June 22, 1941, and two days later occupied Vilna. In this memoir, he describes his life during the subsequent three years until July 1944, when the Soviet army liberated the city. From the very first page, the reader is thrust into the middle of the nightmarish

3 Lazar Engelshtern, *In getos un velder: Fun Vilne biz di Nalibaker vildenis* (Yiddish) (Tel Aviv: Hakibbutz Hameuchad, 1972).

4 Lazar Engelshtern, *Mit di vegn fun der sheyres-hapleyte* (Yiddish) (Tel Aviv: Igud Yotzei Vilna Vehasviva BeYisrael, 1976).

5 Ruth Leimenzon Engles, *Written in a Barn: The Diary of a Young Woman from Vilna* (Jerusalem: Yad Vashem, 2023), p. 165.

experience that my father had already been living through for seventy-five days. In vivid detail, he recounts the amazing story of his Holocaust survival—his escape from the Vilna ghetto to Woronów (Voranava, Voronovo) with the help of an officer in the German army, his truly miraculous escape from a death march, his escape from the Lida ghetto into the forests of Belorussia (Belarus), and his life as a partisan and as chief cook in the Bielski family camp.

As the memoir progresses, snippets of information about my father, his family, and his life are revealed. But these few details are not enough for the reader to form a complete picture of who he was. So, I want to fill in that picture with details about his life before June 22, 1941—details about his family, his experiences, his work, his influences, and the forces that motivated him.

To fully understand the factors that shaped my father, one first needs to understand the prewar environment in which he lived and developed, namely, the Jewish community of Vilna. It was in this city where he was born and grew up, where he received his education, where he worked for several Yiddish newspapers as a compositor, a writer, and a manager, where he became deeply involved in the rich Yiddish cultural life of the Jewish community, and where he got married and had two daughters.

Before its destruction by the Nazis, the Jewish community of Vilna, referred to as the "Jerusalem of Lithuania," was the spiritual hub of Eastern European Jewry. It was a center of traditional Orthodox Judaism, reflecting the legacy of the great Talmudic scholar Rabbi Elijah ben Solomon Zalman, better known as the Vilna Gaon. But Vilna was also a center of secular Jewish intellectual activity, having been one of the most important centers of the Haskala (the Jewish Enlightenment) in Eastern Europe at the beginning of the nineteenth century. It was a community that bustled with Jewish religious and cultural activity, which included educational institutions, newspapers, libraries, theaters, and political parties. It was a community of traditional Orthodox rabbis and gifted Talmudic scholars as well as secular intellectuals, writers, poets, journalists, and educators, all of whom conducted their activities in Yiddish. My father's feelings about this city can best be understood as follows:

> Vilna—the mother of all Jewish cities. A large part of my life was spent in this city. My early childhood, my adolescence and my adult years are all linked with Vilna. I developed and I was molded as a Jew together with this city. The city revealed itself to me slowly, gradually, step by step, courtyard by courtyard, street by street, moment by moment, and now she lives within me, shining with all the colors of the rainbow.[6]

The memory of Vilna continued to be an important factor that influenced his interests and activities throughout his life.

The Engelstern children, 1910.
From left: (back row) Victor, Moshe, and Sarah; (middle row) Rivka and Tybel; (front row) Lazar.

6 Engelshtern, *Mit di vegn*, p. 15.

The Engelstern family, c. 1930.
From left: (back row) Lazar, Moshe, and Rivka's three children Shlomo, Reizel, and Shayna; (front row) Victor, Sarah, Lazar's mother Golda-Feige, and Rivka.

In terms of family life, my father, born in Vilna on April 12, 1902, was the youngest of six children—three boys and three girls. Both the religious and secular components of the Vilna Jewish community were reflected in his family. He grew up and developed within a strong, traditionally Jewish, religious environment, but the Haskala also influenced several members of the family, including himself.

At the age of three, he was sent to study at the *heder*.[7] Both of his grandfathers were rabbis, and his paternal grandfather died when my father was a young child. But his maternal grandfather, who was a learned scholar and had written several books on Jewish Halacha (Jewish law), was a major influence on my father's Yiddishkeit.[8] Some of his fondest

7 A *heder* is a traditional elementary school, teaching the basics of Judaism and the Hebrew language.

8 Yiddishkeit can best be understood in contrast with Judaism. The latter suggests an ideology, a set of definite beliefs like socialism or atheism. Yiddishkeit, on the

memories from childhood were about how he helped his grandfather bake the Passover matza (unleavened bread), keeping track of the precise baking time and then distributing the matzot to the synagogue members. His mother Golda-Feige Ligem Engelstern, a rabbi's daughter, was a religious woman who was very strict in her observance of Jewish Halacha, and so their home was a model of traditional Jewish life. She was also a smart businesswoman who operated a small laundry factory as well as managing several apartments in their courtyard.

The secular influences on my father began when he was sent to the Russian government public school at the age of seven, in addition to attending the *heder*. His father Avraham Engelstern had been a *yeshiva* student before he fell under the influence of the Haskala and left the *yeshiva* before completing his studies. He eventually became a compositor, specializing in printing Russian works. Nevertheless, he always maintained a traditional orthodox perspective and was diligent in his religious observance. He was injured very badly in April 1919, when the Polish army occupied Vilna and carried out a pogrom against the Vilna Jews. He was unable to recover, and he died several months later.

Another family member who played an influential role in my father's life was his brother Moshe, a polymath with broad interests in art, literature, journalism, music, sport, medicine, philosophy, religion, parapsychology, and printing. He followed in his father's footsteps and became a compositor, and for many years he published a weekly Yiddish newspaper. Early in life, he was captured by the revolutionary spirit and was drawn to the Bund,[9] where his activities often got him into trouble with the authorities. It was Moshe who launched my father's career as a compositor in 1921 by getting him his first job at a printing shop, where Moshe knew the owner.

When Vilna came under Polish control in 1921, my father, who was then nineteen years old, spent most of his time hiding from the

other hand, connotes a way of being; not merely a creed but an organic and all-encompassing, pulsing, breathing way of life.

9 The General Jewish Labor Bund in Lithuania, Poland, and Russia, generally called The Bund, was a secular Jewish labor movement predicated on socialism and Jewish nationalism.

Polish military patrols who were grabbing young men on the streets and inducting them into the Polish army. His new job provided a perfect refuge from the Polish military patrols. During the day, he was in the print shop learning the typesetting trade, and after work, he would spend the night keeping watch over the shop, which greatly pleased his boss.

It was during this period that my father developed his great love for the printed Yiddish word. Until then, he had read mostly Russian literature. In his new job, he was immersed in Yiddish writing day and night. During the day, he would set type for various Yiddish books, and at night he would read these Yiddish books that filled the print shop. His feelings about Yiddish writing can be described as follows:

> A new world opened up for me, which until then I had not known. I thirstily drank in the treasures of our classicists and wanted to absorb as much as I could to make up for the years that I had not read Yiddish literature.... From that time on, I read only Yiddish books and became addicted to the printed Yiddish word.[10]

After becoming a qualified compositor, he worked at various print shops in Vilna. He became a member of the printers' union and was eventually elected to the management board, described by him as the "first step into my subsequent many-branched activities in community affairs."[11] During this period, the printers' union grew into a large and important cultural institution in Vilna that, in addition to its professional responsibilities, organized various cultural events such as lectures and political discussions. My father became very involved in both the professional and cultural activities of the union and referred to it as his "second home."[12]

In 1927, my father began to work at the *Vilner Tog* (Vilna Day), one of the major Yiddish newspapers in Vilna. His talents were evidently quickly recognized, as he was promoted to a supervisory position within his first year at the newspaper and a few years later was appointed

10 Engelshtern, *Mit di vegn*, pp. 66–67.

11 Ibid., p. 67.

12 Ibid., p. 70.

to be a manager on the administrative board of the newspaper. After several years as part of the *Vilner Tog* administration, he returned to the typesetting staff, happy to be relieved of dealing with the newspaper's many problems. He continued to work there until the Nazi invasion in June 1941.

During this time before the occupation, my father married Liba Bastomski in November 1931. A year after they got married, their daughter Malkele was born, and two years later they had a second daughter, Taybele. His brother-in-law Shloyme owned a publishing house that published educational books and journals for the evolving Yiddish secular schools. Liba was the administrator of the publishing company. The two important Yiddish journals *Der Haver* (The Friend) and *Grininke Beymelech* (Little Green Trees) were actually administered and edited in their apartment. Their house was always filled with Yiddish literature, newspapers, and periodicals from all over the world. There were also many visitors to their home, people with some kind of interest in the publishing company—teachers, school activists, students, and people from foreign countries as well as the nearby provinces. In this way, my father became acquainted with the elite of Yiddish Vilna.

For ten years, from 1931 to 1941, my father led a happy, meaningful life—at home with his wife and their two little girls, at work as a respected and important member of the newspaper staff, and in the greater Jewish community where he was actively involved in the cultural life of Yiddish Vilna. On June 24, 1941, his happy life was turned upside down and was ended forever when the Nazis occupied Vilna.

David Engles

BETWEEN SURVIVAL AND RESISTANCE: LAZAR ENGELSTERN'S ODYSSEY FROM GHETTOS TO FORESTS

This memoir *Our Partisan Kingdom: From the Vilna Ghetto to the Bielski Family Camp* documents the personal journey of Eliezer (Lazar) Engelstern (1902–1984), later known as Lazar Engles, a Jewish man who endured harrowing experiences, witnessed significant losses, and constantly evaded death during the Holocaust. This is a detailed first-person account of Engelstern's experiences in various ghettos—including the ghettos of Vilna, Woronów, and Lida—until his eventual escape into the forests of Western Belorussia, where he joined the group of partisans commanded by Tuvia Bielski.[1] This

1 The 130-page testimony in Yiddish of Lazar Engelstern was recorded by Yitzhak Alperovich in October 1971 and is currently preserved in the Yad Vashem Archives (YVA), O.3/3608. This publication derives from those firsthand recollections, and other than a few pages at the beginning of the testimony, the two texts are virtually identical.

is the English translation of his memoir, which was first published in Yiddish in 1972 and included a foreword by Yisrael Rudnitzki where he wrote the following:

> One also finds in this book details about the unusual bravery of Jewish youth who undertook a historic mission: to wrest away as many Jewish lives as possible from under the German grip, from the ghettos, and to assemble them and protect them.[2]

Firsthand personal accounts of the Holocaust, narrated by individuals who directly experienced the horrors of the time, provide an invaluable historical record of the atrocities committed during this tragic period. The testimony of a Jewish man who endured the loss of his family, suffered in the ghettos, narrowly escaped death, and later joined a partisan group in the forest offers a profound insight into the multifaceted challenges faced by those targeted by the Nazi regime. His detailed recollections serve as a testament to the enduring resilience and unwavering determination of individuals to survive amid unimaginable adversity, further emphasizing the complexities of life during this tumultuous time. The depth and nuance provided by his personal narrative contribute significantly to a comprehensive understanding of the psychological, emotional, and physical toll exacted by the Holocaust, offering a poignant and humanizing perspective on this dark chapter in history.

Escape from Vilna

Vilna was home to numerous Jewish institutions that focused on education, culture, libraries, research, religion, welfare, and more. The Germans conquered the city on June 24, 1941, following the Nazi invasion of the Soviet Union known as Operation Barbarossa. At that time, Vilna had approximately 60,000 Jewish residents. Shortly after their arrival, the Germans began implementing policies of persecution and discrimination. Educational institutions saw classes canceled and

2 Engelshtern, *In getos un velder*, p. 8.

teachers dismissed. Jews were required to wear yellow badges with the letter "J" sewn in the center. There was also property confiscation and theft of valuables. These actions were conducted by the Germans with the collaboration of the Lithuanians.

The Vilna ghetto was established on Saturday, September 6, 1941, in the old Jewish quarter. Thousands of Jews were murdered during the ghetto's formation as violent *Aktionen* were carried out against them. They were forcibly expelled from their homes and had to walk to the ghetto, carrying their belongings. Two ghettos were established in the city: a larger one (Ghetto I) with 30,000 Jews, and a smaller one (Ghetto II) with between 9,000 and 11,000 Jews. Thousands of Jews were taken to the notorious Lukiškės (Lukiszki) Prison that day, and over the following days, around 6,000 Jews were brought to Ponary where they were shot dead.[3] Extreme overcrowding prevailed in the ghettos, and violent *Aktionen* continued to occur.

With the stabilization of life in the ghetto, residents began to create a semblance of cultural life, including theater, sports, an active library, an education system, music, and more. The Judenrat (Jewish Council) and the Jewish police were established to manage life within the ghetto. From July 1942, the Judenrat was led by Jacob Gens, who headed a strong and authoritative council. Additionally, underground organizations were formed with the aim of actively resisting the Germans, either through rebellion within the ghetto or by fleeing to the surrounding forests.

Lazar Engelstern's memoir begins the day before the deportation of the Jews of Vilna to the ghetto, immediately immersing the reader into the heartrending recollections of that day. The narrative portrays the traumatic journey of Engelstern and his family as they were uprooted from their home and compelled to relocate to the confines of

3 Ponary (Paneriai) was the main mass murder site of the Vilna Jews. It is located about 11 kilometers southeast of Vilna. The Nazis used the pits that were dug there as a site for the extermination of around 70,000 people, mostly Jews but also Poles who were anti-Nazis, Soviet prisoners of war, Lithuanian priests, and Roma. Executions by shooting, in what is known as the "Holocaust by Bullets," took place there for three years between July 1941 and July 1944.

the ghetto. Through his individual perspective, readers are confronted with the agonizing reality of this transition and the distressing scenes of overcrowded apartments, where individuals struggled to navigate the cramped spaces among strangers. As Engelstern's account unfolds, the stark realities of daily life in the ghetto become palpable, depicting the adaptation to the dire circumstances that became the new norm. Additionally, his role as a father takes center stage, offering an intimate portrayal of his relentless struggle to protect and provide for his children amid the unforgiving backdrop of the ghetto's brutality. Historian Aharon Einat wrote in his book *Hayei Yom-Yom Begeto Vilna* (Daily Life in the Vilna Ghetto):

> The first night in the ghetto was especially traumatic for the Jews of Vilna and was scratched deep in their memory. After the crisis of the abandonment of homes and property, after all the horrors of the road and the hardships of finding a place to live, and in the shadow of the fragmented news of the loss of family members and acquaintances, they found themselves cut off from their former lives, crammed together to the point of horror in foreign apartments, with unfamiliar people.[4]

In his descriptive and informative narrative, Engelstern vividly depicts the menace of the *chapunes* (grabbers). These Lithuanian collaborators were notorious for abducting Jewish men from the streets of Vilna and herding them toward the grim fate awaiting them at the death site of Ponary.

He tells of the rescue attempts by Anton Schmid, an Austrian Wehrmacht soldier who helped Jews from various ghettos, including Vilna. Born in 1900 in Vienna, Schmid was stationed in Vilna in 1941 and headed a military unit called Versprengten-Sammelstelle—the unit responsible for reassigning soldiers who had been separated from their units. His office was near the train station in Vilna, and from there he witnessed the persecution and murder of the Jews. He used German

4 Aharon Einat, *Hayei Yom-Yom Begeto Vilna* (Hebrew) (Haifa: Moreshet, 2013), p. 100.

military vehicles to smuggle Jews out of the city—where the danger was especially great—to places that were relatively quiet at the time, including Woronów to where Engelstern was smuggled.

Engelstern recalls this unexpected rescue, describing the dramatic moment of getting into Schmid's truck together with his wife Liba, their six-year-old daughter Taybel, and many others: "Everything happened so unexpectedly! We were focused so exclusively on finding some way—any way—to get out of our desperate situation that we never even gave a single thought to where we were being taken." Indeed, upon arriving in Woronów, he wrote: "In Vilna, there were Nazi murderers, death, and devastation, and here, it felt like a Garden of Eden."

A Refugee in Woronów

At the beginning of the war, there were approximately 1,000 Jews in Woronów. The town was conquered by the Germans on June 26–27, 1941, and during that summer, a ghetto was established. Jews were subjected to forced labor, robbery, and abuse. Executions were also carried out by the German authorities. Refugees from the Vilna ghetto managed to reach Woronów, hoping to find refuge there.

The Jewish residents of Woronów extended a warm welcome to these newcomers, despite the enormous risks they faced by aiding these "illegal" guests. However, this fragile sanctuary would soon crumble when the Germans, with the assistance of local collaborators, relentlessly pursued and apprehended those Jews who had arrived in Woronów from Vilna. On November 6, 1941, a large group of Vilna Jews was herded into the movie theater building. They were subsequently transported to the Zamkowy Forest, where they met a horrific end. Engelstern's wife and young daughter Taybel were among those murdered.[5]

5 The final major *Aktion* in Woronów unfolded in May 1942. On May 11, a substantial force comprised of German and Lithuanian personnel entered the ghetto, and a few days later, they assembled the Jewish inhabitants in the market square. There, they were forced to kneel and surrender all their remaining valuables, jewelry, and money to the assailants. A selection process ensued,

Narrowly escaping death, Engelstern managed to flee alone from the Woronów ghetto before this *Aktion*, traversing fields and forests until he reached Lida, located about 35 kilometers south of Woronów. There, he was assigned to work at the German police headquarters—in his words, "Right in the midst of the murderers themselves."

Persecution in the Lida Ghetto

At the outbreak of World War II, about 6,300 Jews lived in Lida—about a third of the city's residents. When the Germans arrived in Lida on June 25, 1941, a significant battle ensued, resulting in extensive bombing and destruction of the city. By June 28, Lida had been conquered by the Germans. A Judenrat was established, and the Jews were forced into labor to clear the destruction caused by the bombing. In December 1941, the Jews were deported to a ghetto situated in the city's poorest streets, where overcrowding prevailed. Several hundred refugees from Vilna and other locations smuggled themselves into the ghetto, where the abuse and persecution of the Jews continued.

After his arrival in Lida, Engelstern was shattered by the devastating news of his wife and daughter's demise and clung to the possibility that his other daughter Malka might still be alive in the Vilna ghetto, providing him with a glimmer of hope amid the despair. The memoir graphically portrays the brutal and violent actions of the Germans in Lida, illustrating their abuse of the Jewish population and their ruthless confiscation of all property and valuables. The Judenrat was obligated to comply with the Germans' demands. Additionally, he

separating a group of approximately 600–700 professionals from the rest of the Jews. The remaining Jews were detained in the square without access to food or drink while nearby peasants dug large pits in a forest. The Germans then forced the Jews to run to the execution site, where approximately 1,834 individuals were tragically shot. This devastating *Aktion* was overseen by the regional commissar Rudolf Werner. The few hundred professionals who managed to survive this ordeal were subsequently transferred to the Lida ghetto.

describes how the local Poles and White Russians collaborated in the persecution and mistreatment of the Jewish community:

> The White-Russian police made sure that everyone worked diligently, giving these bosses an opportunity to harass the Jews and extort money and other valuable items from them. It was much harder to bear the suffering from these local hooligans than from the Germans. The pain in our hearts was even greater because, after all, they were local Poles who until recently had been our neighbors.

The abuse of the Jews reached a key peak when one Sunday—meant to be a day of rest from work—the Germans gathered around 500 men, including Engelstern, and forced them to chase and catch rabbits in the freezing, snow-covered forest. They were inadequately dressed and faced the threat of being shot should they fail to fulfill the task. This incident is described in chilling detail and is a stark example of the Nazis' brutality and abuse of the Jews.

On May 8, 1942, a murderous *Aktion* took place in the Lida ghetto, during which the Jews were gathered and the perpetrators selected who would live and who would die. Engelstern recalls: "The entire group of Jews—over 5,000 men, women, and children—sat there like condemned prisoners, resigned and with glazed eyes, waiting for the Hitlerists to free them from this hell on Earth."

He expressively describes the heart-wrenching scenes of families torn apart, capturing the agony of reluctant goodbyes and the overwhelming despair that permeated each separation. Through his narrative, he provides a detailed picture of the cynical selection process, sharing intimate conversations he overheard among those deliberating their fates and contemplating their next move. Amid the chaos and panic, his recollections reveal notable instances of courage, resistance, and defiance among the condemned Jews.

Fortunately, he managed to survive the *Aktion* by slipping away from a convoy of people who were being led to a mass murder site, astutely feigning death until the convoy had moved on. After recovering from this distressing escape with the help of local peasants,

Engelstern received news of the appalling massacre that had claimed the lives of the majority of Lida's Jews. In response, he resolved to return to the depleted ghetto, where he encountered refugees—among them Orthodox, observant Jews—from the town of Radun.[6]

Among the survivors of this deadly *Aktion*, aware of the grim fate that awaited them, a debate arose: Should they seek refuge in the nearby forests or remain within the confines of the ghetto? At this point, initial encounters with the partisans began, and "contact between the forest and the ghetto increased with each passing day."

Into the Forest: A Testament of Survival with the Bielski Partisans

Shortly after the German invasion of the Soviet Union in June 1941, the Soviet partisan movement emerged in the Eastern European forests to resist the Nazi occupation. The partisan movement did not gain significant traction until the spring and summer of 1942. During this period, a partisan high command was established under the leadership of Marshal Kliment Yefremovich Voroshilov (1881–1969), a distinguished Soviet military officer and politician who was appointed as the commander in chief.

This movement engaged in activities such as intelligence gathering, sabotage, and targeted attacks against the German army.

6 Radun (Radin) is a village located 90 kilometers west of Minsk. Prior to the war, approximately 900–1,000 Jews resided in the town. The epicenter of Radun's Jewish spiritual life was the renowned *yeshiva*, established in 1869 by Yisrael Meir Kagen, famously known as the Chafetz Chaim. In late June 1941, German forces occupied the town, and on November 16, they established a fenced-off ghetto, confining over 2,000 Jews within its boundaries, including refugees and Jews from the surrounding villages. In January 1942, a denunciation led to the execution of approximately forty Jews, including Lipa Skolski, the head of the ghetto's Jewish police, along with his family. On Friday, May 8, 1942, the ghetto was besieged, and it was liquidated a few days later, resulting in the murder of around 1,000 Jews. Approximately 300 people managed to escape and seek refuge in the nearby forests.

Those Jews in ghettos who were members of underground organizations sought to establish contact with the partisans, hoping to join their ranks as a means of survival and resistance. Among the Jews who reached the partisans and successfully integrated, some took up arms and participated actively in combat, while others contributed through support roles such as cooking, laundry, and other essential tasks to sustain the fighting force. Tensions occasionally surfaced between combatants and noncombatants regarding the recognition of their contributions to the partisan effort. This dynamic underscores the complex nature of resistance movements and the diverse roles individuals played in the collective struggle against the Nazis and is portrayed in this memoir.

Engelstern made the decision to flee the Lida ghetto for the nearby forests in spring 1943, and he recounts the dramatic night when he and a large group of Jews successfully escaped with the assistance of the ghetto's Jewish police.[7] Upon arrival in the forests, he joined the partisan group led by Tuvia Bielski and his brothers, and a new phase of his life unfolded.

Regarding the establishment of this partisan group, at the end of 1941 the Bielski brothers and other family members roamed between villages and towns, seeking shelter with the help of farmers' acquaintances. Their parents had been tragically murdered during an *Aktion* in the Nowogródek (Novogrudok) ghetto on December 7–8, 1941. By May 1942, the surviving family members gathered in a nearby forest and decided to establish a partisan camp. Tuvia, the eldest brother and a natural-born leader, was chosen as the commander. His primary goal was to increase the camp's population, believing that preserving the lives of the few remaining Jews was paramount despite the challenges of securing sufficient food for a large group. The partisan camp grew as more Jews who had managed to escape from ghettos joined, expanding the community under Tuvia's leadership.[8]

7 In the spring of 1943, many Jews escaped the Lida ghetto, and hundreds of them joined the Bielski partisans. Most Jews came to the forests unarmed. See Yitzhak Arad, *In the Shadow of the Red Banner: Soviet Jews in the War against Nazi Germany* (Jerusalem: Gefen Publishing House and Yad Vashem, 2010), p. 297.

8 For further reading on the Bielski partisans, see Nechama Tec, *Defiance: The Bielski*

He recalls that "Tuvia Bielski's partisan camp was a unique amalgamation–part family camp and part combat *otriad* [partisan group]. Every Jewish woman, regardless of her age, was both accepted and on an equal footing under the protection of the Bielski *otriad*."[9] Indeed, the Bielski partisan camp comprised Jews from diverse backgrounds and ages, mainly hailing from small Jewish towns and villages. Despite facing bereavement and adversity, the Jewish community that crystalized in the camp demonstrated both a remarkable resilience and a tenacious will to survive in the challenging forest setting.

This memoir presents a valuable account of partisan life in the Bielski *otriad*, including their combat activities as well as the revenge acts of the Jewish partisans against local peasants who were collaborators with the Nazis. He also describes the antisemitic tendencies and actions of the Russian and White-Russian partisans toward their Jewish counterparts, who tried to find ways to harm Jews and steal their scarce possessions. "More than one Jew paid with his life for trying to resist… The life of a Jewish partisan meant nothing to them." He also refers to the relations between the partisans and the local peasants: Some of them were kind and supportive, whereas others denounced partisans to the German authorities and even murdered them. While the local peasants were a source of food and supplies for the partisans, they also had to provide the Germans with rations of their produce, so they "were caught between a hammer and an anvil."

A dramatic tale told in this memoir is the escape from a massive German blockade against the partisans in the Naliboki Forest. In July

Partisans (New York: Oxford University Press, 1993); Peter Duffy, *The Bielski Brothers: The True Story of Three Men Who Defied the Nazis, Saved 1200 Jews, and Built a Village in the Forest* (New York: HarperCollins, 2003); Jack Kagan and Dov Cohen, *Surviving the Holocaust with the Russian Jewish Partisans* (London: Vallentine Mitchell, 1998); Allan Levine, *Fugitives of the Forest: The Heroic Story of Jewish Resistance and Survival during the Second World War* (Toronto: Stoddart, 1998); Chaya Bielski, *Haru'ah Hahaya: Partizanim B'gedud Ha'ahim Bielski* (Hebrew) (Jerusalem: Yad Vashem, 2012).

9 *Otriad* is a Russian word referring to a division of the partisan fighting forces in the forest. Here and throughout the book, it refers to the partisan groups, both Russian and Jewish, that were organized in the forests to fight against the Nazi occupiers.

and August 1943, the Germans conducted Operation Hermann,[10] during which they burned villages, murdered partisans and others, and sent some to forced labor camps. The Bielski partisans managed to find shelter in a swamp area and were thus saved.

In the Bielski partisan unit, Engelstern assumed the role of chief cook for the base. His memoir provides beautiful descriptions of daily life in the camp—about both the physical work and the cultural activities that took place there: from the construction of the *zemlyankas* (partisan bunkers), cooking, and laundering, to the coordination of social and cultural gatherings, musical performances and education, and more.

Evenings were often dedicated to fireside gatherings, where the group sang songs in various languages including Hebrew, Yiddish, and Russian, creating a festive atmosphere within the camp as night descended. The art of storytelling was also cherished, with members sharing tales with one another. As Engelstern reflects: "The storyteller's objective [was] to elicit laughter, laughter if only with tears, but nonetheless laughter, and to forget about the sad yesterdays and the uncertain tomorrows for a while."

The communal sleeping arrangements within the *zemlyankas*—with several individuals sharing a single bench—were quite cramped and demanded considerable patience among the inhabitants. "We slept like herrings tightly packed in a can," Engelstern recalls. These shared moments deep in the forests felt like an escape to a different world and fostered a sense of camaraderie. According to Engelstern: "No one was in a hurry to go to sleep in the cold huts, so we would sit around the fire late into the night. These evenings would put us in a better mood and helped us to forget our troubles."

The Bielski partisan *otriad*—or the Bielski family camp as it included women, children, and the elderly—operated as a self-sustaining community akin to a small town. "The base took on the appearance

10 Operation Hermann was a large-scale anti-partisan operation carried out by Nazi German forces in the Naliboki Forest area of Belorussia in 1943. The operation aimed to eliminate Soviet partisan groups in the region, which had become a significant center of resistance against the German occupation.

of a typical Jewish *shtetl*.[11] And, indeed, soon the town was given the name Belsk, after the Bielskis." Skilled individuals, such as tailors, carpenters, shoemakers, blacksmiths, hatmakers, watchmakers, and others contributed to the well-being of the community. They constructed essential facilities, including a sausage factory, a steam bathhouse for cleanliness, and a hospital where they effectively managed epidemics and coped with other challenging health concerns.

Pregnancy and childbirth presented sensitive and complex challenges within the partisan camps in the forests. Women often took measures to avoid pregnancy due to the harsh conditions and the lack of medical care. Abortions, when carried out, were conducted under primitive and perilous circumstances. Those who did give birth occasionally entrusted their newborns to the care of farmers or acquaintances outside the camp, hoping to ensure their safety until the war's end. This arrangement was seen as a temporary solution, allowing children a chance of survival amid the uncertainty and danger of wartime. Notably, Engelstern delves into this unique experience of women within the partisan units, shedding light on the complex topics of abortions and births that occurred in the forests with specific reference to the Bielski camp. He describes the care of over 100 children who found refuge in the Bielski partisan camp. He writes:

> The children brought a ray of happiness into the gloomy atmosphere of concern about tomorrow and the future...We guarded this treasure with great care...And it was not just their parents who cherished them. The commander made a concerted effort to ensure that the children had enough to eat and that they could enjoy a normal childhood while in the forest. This was especially the case for those whose parents were no longer alive.

He also provides insights into both the hierarchical structure among the partisans and the dynamics between the commanders and the

11 *Shtetl* is the Yiddish term for a town, commonly referring to small market towns in pre-World War II Eastern Europe with a large Yiddish-speaking Jewish population.

general populace. As he states, "men who owned a rifle had the highest standing."

Concerning discipline among the partisans, those found guilty of violating regulations faced severe punishment under the court-martial standards adopted from the Soviet army. This could include the death penalty. For instance, misplacing a weapon in combat or falling asleep during guard duty were offenses that could result in execution. The author relays an account about an "unusual event" that occurred in the partisan base. A small *zemlyanka* was designated to be the camp prison, where members who broke the law were incarcerated, and the controversial affair was the execution of one of the leading partisans, Israel Kesler, by the Bielski brothers. Kesler was accused of treason and was shot to death. "I only remember that this tragic incident shocked us deeply," he concludes.

In a picturesque, descriptive, fluent, and captivating manner, Engelstern's memoir about his Holocaust experiences shares not only what he personally saw and endured but also provides crucial details that enhance our comprehension of the historical context. Such accounts carry immense significance and provide a deeply human portrayal of the Holocaust, revealing the experiences, emotions, and struggles of those who were not in positions of authority or influence. From this unique vantage point, Engelstern's memoir goes beyond the traditional top-down approach and delves into the lives of individuals whose stories offer an intimate look at the resilience and determination of those who found themselves caught in the midst of unimaginable horrors.

What makes this memoir particularly compelling is the lens through which it views history. Rather than focusing solely on the grand narratives and major players of the Holocaust, this account sheds light on the overlooked, the everyday, and seemingly insignificant moments that collectively form a mosaic of survival, resistance, and hope. Indeed, this book contributes to a more comprehensive understanding of the Holocaust.

Daniela Ozacky Stern

FOREWORD TO THE YIDDISH EDITION

Lazar Engelstern was born in Vilna in 1902. For many years, he was immersed in the world of lead letters, working as a typesetter for the Kletskin Publishing Company as well as the newspaper *Vilner Tog*. He was a member of Vilna's creative Jewish community, but he only took up his pen when the call for Jews to "write it down" reached him, by which point, Jewish Vilna had already been silenced, imprisoned in a ghetto, with thousands of victims swallowed up in the graves of Ponary.

In his notebook, he wrote: "Seventy-five days have passed in pain and pogrom-terror, with the expectation that at any minute something ominous would happen. The Nazis do not give us any time to catch our breath." He later writes: "The ghetto might be a relief. Maybe, one would not feel so abandoned there." From these restrained first sentences, we immediately recognize the terrible reality and the nightmare of those days and nights.

These first few brief notes together with the hundreds of pages carved into his memory have now been gathered together into this book in order to fulfill the pledge to tell the world about the Nazi atrocities, about his own suffering and struggles during the years of the destruction. He did this responsibly, writing only about what he himself had seen and experienced.

In this memoir, Engelstern recounts the German crimes and the ghetto slaughters, incidents that directly involved him and his family, in the unvarnished language of an eyewitness report, stripped of the tragic fog that is the state of his own soul as he relives the gruesome past. It is only later, in the parts titled "Where Do We Get Weapons?" and "Proud and Fearless," as well as in the entire forest epic, that the descriptions are full of sublime moments, emotional unloading, charming humor, and all expressed with great literary skill. In the description of Tuvia Bielski's partisan group, he avoids an extensive portrayal of the various actions carried out against the German occupiers in which his *otriad*[1] companions took part and excelled, simply because he did not participate in them. He was among those without weapons who, in his own way, contributed to the battle against the enemy.

One also finds in this book details about the unusual bravery of Jewish youth who undertook a historic mission: to wrest away as many Jewish lives as possible from under the German grip, from the ghettos, and to assemble them and protect them, referring to those men who could not join the Soviet partisan *otriads*—because they had no weapons and for other reasons—as well as women and children. Lazar Engelstern tells us about the daring exploits of this "bunch of *malbushim*,"[2] who were deep in the forest behind enemy lines, adding a marvelous chapter to the story of the Jewish resistance movement.

First and foremost, however, this memoir is an account about the fate of a Jewish family under German occupation. Lazar Engelstern's purpose is to tell us about both himself and his nearest and dearest whom he lost along the long road of suffering. His purpose is to tell us

1 As mentioned earlier, an *otriad* was a division of the partisan fighting forces in the forest.

2 *Malbush* (pl. *malbushim*) is a Hebrew word meaning a piece of clothing. This term was a derogatory term that was used in the Bielski camp to refer to people who did not have a weapon and were not fighters.

about his first attempt to escape death in the Vilna ghetto followed by his later escapes from the Woronów slaughter and subsequently from the killing field in the Lida ghetto, and ultimately about how he arrived at the "Shtetl Belsk" in the Naliboki wilderness—how he reached the forest that meant salvation, all alone, as the last surviving member of his family.

Yisrael Rudnitzki

CHAPTER ONE

FROM VILNA TO WORONÓW

Day and Night

Vilna, September 5, 1941[1]

It is the seventy-fifth day living under the heel of the Nazi occupation. Seventy-five days have passed in pain and pogrom-terror, with the expectation that at any minute something ominous could happen. The Nazis do not give us any time to catch our breath. Sometimes, one barely has time to find out about a decree that has recently been issued when already a new decree has been passed and

1 The Germans transferred the Vilna Jews to the ghetto the next day, on September 6, 1941. Around 40,000 Jews were crammed into the two ghettos that had been established in the city in an area that had previously housed less than 10,000 people. Since the first day of the Nazi occupation of Vilna on June 24, 1941, the Nazis together with their Lithuanian helpers had already murdered almost 20,000 Jews. Over the next several months, many thousands more were annihilated.

is being spread by word of mouth. Apparently, they know what they are doing, confusing our minds, keeping us in suspense, upsetting our nerves, and turning us into spiritual cripples, so it will be easier for them to carry out their diabolical plans. Fifteen thousand Jewish men have been torn away from their homes, and to where they have disappeared—no one knows.

The days drag on forever. During each day, I wish for night to arrive. Perhaps then I'll be able to fall asleep, so my mind can get some rest. When night does eventually arrive, I take to my bed. I lie in the dark with my eyes open, and instead of sleeping, I relive the events of that day. My head hurts from thinking. The nights drag on forever too. Every once in a while, my eyes stray to the window, seeking a ray of the dawn's light. I always want the nights to end and for the dark thoughts that have tormented me all night to disappear. A dim ray of light pushes itself through the curtained window, the sign that a new day is approaching, and it is often at this moment that my eyes close, and I fall asleep.

We are already quite familiar with the early morning ring at the gate, bringing the *chapunes* (grabbers)—the Lithuanian Ypatingasis būrys, the "chosen ones"—to whom the Nazi authorities of occupied Vilna have handed over the job of catching Jewish men. The captured men have never been seen or heard from again. Oh, how many times have I almost fallen into the hands of the *chapunes* before managing to escape to a hiding place at the last moment? Each morning, when the inevitable ring at the gate wakes me up, quick as a cat, before the building janitor even opens the gate, I spring up the steps to my prepared hideout in the attic, pull up the ladder behind me, and hide. I lie there, my body contorted into a ball, until I receive the signal from Liba, my wife, that it is safe to come down.

* * *

It was in this way that the pain-filled days and sleepless nights stretched on, waiting to be confined in a ghetto. We actually wished that this would happen already—the sooner the better. The ghetto might be a relief. Maybe, one would not feel so abandoned there. On that day, more and more rumors had been circulating about the ghetto, and news was spreading that the ghetto was now ready.

That night—September 5, 1941—actually turned out to be a calm one. At daybreak, there was no ring at the gate by the *chapunes*. Exhausted from so many sleepless nights, we fell into a deep sleep before two loud knocks at the door woke us abruptly. We jumped out of our beds, terrified that death was at hand. My wife went to open the door. Two Lithuanian military personnel pushed their way into the house and harshly ordered us to be ready to vacate the house and go down to the courtyard in half an hour. We could take with us whatever we wanted.

Our family consisted of five people: myself, my wife, my two little daughters—aged eight and five—and my sister-in-law Malke Haymson-Bastomski, who had been living with us since the Nazis occupied Vilna. Her husband, Shloyme Bastomski,[2] had the good fortune of dying following an operation two months prior to the Nazi occupation of Vilna.

In our minds, even though we were prepared to be imprisoned in a ghetto, this abrupt order so confused us that, for a while, we remained frozen to the spot. However, we quickly recovered and realized that we did not have another moment to waste if we were to have enough time to take at least some things with us, the most essential items. My wife began to get the children dressed, while my sister-in-law and I began to prepare the things we needed to take with us. When I ran over to the closets full of clothing and underwear, I quickly became disoriented and couldn't decide which items to take first. I kept looking at my watch and filling the suitcases with whatever my hands landed upon. As if in a deliberately vindictive manner, the hands of the clock kept moving ever so quickly.

We had not yet managed to fill the suitcases when the same two military personnel reappeared and ordered us to leave the apartment

2 Shloyme Bastomski (1891–1941) was a Yiddish pedagogue, folklorist, writer and editor, and a pioneer of Yiddish secular schooling. Bastomski was a member of the Socialist Zionist movement. He established one of the most productive Yiddish educational publishing houses, Di Naye Yidishe Folkshul (The New Yiddish Elementary School). Both Shloyme and his wife Malke did not survive the war.

immediately and to leave the keys behind. We took one last look at our home and at the possessions that we had accumulated over the many years of hard work and effort. Now, we were abandoning it all.

It was not until we had our suitcases in our hands and had begun to leave the house that our children first started to cry, their frightened voices cutting even deeper into our anguished hearts. Their young little hearts sensed that they would never again have such a good home. The Lithuanians stood by cold-bloodedly and waited until we emerged from the building. Outside in the courtyard, we met all our neighbors. Each one was burdened with suitcases and bundles of bedding, their backs bowing under the heavy load.

We lived at 24 Stepono Street, at the corner of Šopeno Street, and so it was our good fortune that we only had to walk one block to reach the partially finished ghetto on Rudnicka Street. Jews from other parts of the city had to drag their things with great anguish and difficulty across the city, in the great heat that just happened to occur that day. But we, too, were extremely shaken from just walking that single block, laden with heavy bundles on our shoulders, passing between a cordon of uniformed Lithuanians who were standing several rows deep on both sides of the street.

The local Christian population filled the sidewalks, looking on with delight as the Jews were being driven into the ghetto. Soon, they would be able to appropriate Jewish homes together with all their contents. After all, they had dreamed about this for many years. Such was the horrible scene when a man—a brute—suddenly jumped out from the mass of Christian onlookers, snatched a bundle from one of the Jews, and escaped undisturbed.

As we were pushed along this stream of humankind toward the ghetto gate on Rudnicka Street, I immediately realized that there was not a minute to waste: we needed to find ourselves an apartment. I went from one courtyard to another, up and down the stairs, but in each place, I was met with the same refrain: "There is no longer any room here." Exhausted, I returned to where I had left my wife and children. That was when I found out about our good luck. My sister-in-law Malke Haymson, despite her diminished strength, had also gone in search of a place to stay, and she was fortunate to find space in an apartment of one of her students from the Real Gymnasium,[3] located at 14 Rudnicka Street. As soon as the student's mother saw Malke, she invited her to stay, even though there were already eighteen people living in the apartment that in total consisted of just two small rooms and a kitchen, separated by a folding screen. With our family of five, we were now twenty-three altogether. At that moment, we felt like this was a great piece of luck! People were wandering through the streets and courtyards, walking on the filthy cobblestones with their bundles, whereas at least now we had a roof over our heads.

View of a busy street in the Vilna ghetto.
Photo Collection, Yad Vashem Archives (YVA),
Borowicz Collection, 3380/582.

3 The Real Gymnasium was a Jewish community high school in which classes were taught in Yiddish, under the auspices of the Tsentraler Bildung Komitet (Central Education Committee), which promoted Yiddish secular education in Vilna. It was located in the courtyard of 6 Rudnicka Street. In 1933, it received government recognition, and from then on, the matriculation exams enabled the graduates to enroll in the university. In September 1941, the Judenrat (Jewish Council) of Ghetto I settled in the Real Gymnasium's building.

When the time came for sleep, our spirits darkened and dismay set in. As we were the last ones to move into the apartment, only a small space remained for us on the floor near the door. There was barely enough room for us to lie down. But this was a minor problem, and we managed to squeeze in somehow. Things got worse during the night when the neighbors had to take care of their needs, and since it was dark, they kept stepping on us. By the following night, however, we had become accustomed to it.

We could hardly wait to go out onto the street and into the courtyard of the Real Gymnasium, which fate had decreed would become the residence of the despised Judenrat (Jewish Council). It was precisely here, between the walls of this exemplary Jewish educational institution, where heartrending scenes would play out. I spotted my mother amid the dense mass of people. Tears began to run down our faces. Shortly after, she told me the tragic news.

Before moving to the ghetto, my mother had lived on Šnipiškės Street with my sister, her husband, and her three children—a boy and two girls. During the move to the ghetto, my mother ended up on Rudnicka Street, while my sister and her two daughters were forcibly driven to Lidzka Street. She told me that during the night, the murderous Lithuanian helpers had taken 2,000 Jews from there to Lukiškės Prison and then to Ponary.[4] My sister's husband—my brother-in-law—together with their sixteen-year-old son had been caught by the *chapunes* during the first few days of the German occupation. The same fate had befallen my eldest brother Moshe. My father had already been dead for twenty years.

After crying over the terrible news of the last few days, I brought my mother to our little corner. Now, we were twenty-four in the apartment. That evening, we squeezed together a little closer, and the night passed. After this, however, my mother said to me: "My son, in any event, I do not have long to live, so I am going back to Šnipiškės Street. I hope I will find a place to stay among the

4 Lukiškės (Lukiszki) Prison was the place where the captured Jews were imprisoned in rough conditions before they were taken to the murder site of Ponary, mostly by trucks.

Christian neighbors of our courtyard with whom I always got along well as a good neighbor." I only saw her once more after that, shortly before we escaped from the ghetto.

On our second day in the ghetto, my wife was in despair. In the confusion of our sudden departure from our home, she had forgotten to take the abundant amount of food that had been prepared earlier, and we did not even have a pot or a teakettle. So, at first, there was no warm water for the children. In addition, an order of priority had been established for using the single kitchen. Those who had a pot were the first to cook. Therefore, my wife had to wait until someone had a pot that was no longer being used, and it was the good mother of my sister-in-law's student who provided us with a pot. So, we ate very late at night when the line had dwindled. By the next day, this inconvenience was already considered normal.

Our Escape from the Ghetto

Shortly after our arrival in the ghetto, I began work at the train station. It seemed that the easiest work in the ghetto could be found there, and I also received a much-coveted work permit. But when the Nazis began to play mind games with the colors of such permits—introducing white passes, specialist passes, passes with a "good" stamp, and so on—I began to move around and change jobs, like everyone else was doing.[5] My work was always in the train station, until one day, a German from the train depot, a Nazi and a murderer, beat me so badly that I barely escaped with my life. After that experience, I searched in every way possible for an indoor job, and I found one. Thanks to this incident, a small benefit resulted for my wife and two little girls—some thick soup.

5 Both men and women were required to work in the ghetto, but they had to have work permits, also referred to as passes or *Scheinen*. Without a pass, one was a prime candidate to be sent to Ponary. The Germans kept changing the form and the color of the passes that were considered valid. The term "mind games" refers to the Germans' constant revisions of what was considered a valid pass.

Near the train station, there was a kitchen where, all day long, large pots of soup were cooked for those soldiers passing through Vilna on their way to the front. This kitchen was managed by some German women, and Jews from the ghetto worked there as forced laborers. I got a job there as a woodcutter. Several Jews worked in the kitchen, washing pots and doing other chores. They had more than enough soup for themselves, and they took care to make sure that those on the outside also got some soup. But on the days when only a few soldiers came to the kitchen, it was like a holiday for us. We all gorged ourselves on soup. I was thrifty with my portion, and during the time that I worked there, my family also benefited from the thick soup, and they no longer had to make use of the narrow kitchen.

But what good was the soup if the job didn't come with the right kind of work permit with the German stamp ensuring one's life, a permit that people clamored tooth and nail for in the hope that it would enable them to survive? So, I left the woodcutting job—and the soup—and began to search again for a "good" job with a secure work permit. At this point, a path was marked out for me, a path that would eventually lead to my escape from the ghetto at the time of the Yellow Pass Decree.[6]

At first, I fell in with a group of bookbinders, who made the darkening material for the windows of the train station as well as for neighboring buildings that had been taken over by the Germans. We tidied up a side corner of the large tunnel that led to the platforms and set up a laboratory for the preparation of both the black paper and the hanging racks. We were in virtual paradise in this tunnel: There

6 When the ghetto was first established, there was no limit to the number of work permits (*Scheinen*) that could be issued. However, the Nazis subsequently implemented a new system, and only 3,000 work permits were issued in the form of yellow passes. The yellow passes granted immunity to the holder and to three members of their family—a spouse and two children up to the age of sixteen. This allowed for a maximum of 12,000 Jews to be protected by the yellow passes. At the time, the ghetto totaled almost 28,000 inhabitants, so 16,000 Jews were left without passes. This decree became known as the Yellow Pass Decree. On October 24, 1941, most of these 16,000 Jews were taken to Ponary and were murdered. This became known as the Yellow Pass *Aktion*. There were two such *Aktionen*: The first was on October 24, 1941, and the second on November 3–4, 1941.

were no Germans to deal with, and no one bossed us around. We were considered specialists who made "useful" things, but to us, this preparation of darkening material was so insignificant. In addition to the fact that we were not being watched, there was another important benefit. From time to time one of us would slip outside and score some food from a Christian. In the tunnel, we would somehow camouflage the food, and then little by little, when it was safe to do so at the ghetto gate, we would bring it into the ghetto hidden in the cuffs of our pants.

Document inspection by the Gestapo at the Rudnicka Street entrance of the Vilna ghetto, October 24, 1941. Photo Collection, YVA, 1044/148.

My greatest joy was when I had the opportunity to purchase some apples for my children from a Christian. My older daughter Malkele was eight years old at the time, and the younger one Taybele was nearly six. Like all the other children of the same age in the ghetto, they understood quite well what was happening to us, and in their own way, they suffered alongside their mother and father. But what could compare to their joy when I managed to sneak in a few apples in the cuffs of my pants? When I gave them each an apple, they would not eat it immediately, first holding it in their thin little hands, shifting it from one hand to the other, refraining from eating it all at once. Their mother would then cut the apples into slices, which they would eat slowly.

Following this job preparing darkening materials in the tunnel, my life's path led me to a job at 15 Kolejowa Street, which incidentally became my last job in the Vilna ghetto. Situated across the street from the train station, 15 Kolejowa Street had actually been the last-known address of my brother-in-law Shloyme Bastomski, and it happened to be my fate to work in precisely this apartment for a sergeant in the German army who would later become my savior.

Several dozen Jews from the ghetto did various jobs in this work unit: paper-hangers, carpenters, locksmiths, and others. But when the Yellow Pass Decree came into effect and we found out what awaited us, everyone began to use every means possible to obtain a yellow pass. However, it became clear that I had no chance of receiving a yellow pass because very few such passes had been distributed to my work unit. Only the most "necessary" Jews would be able to continue working, and they would be the ones to receive the yellow passes.

At this point, I began to look for a way to save myself and my family. Before I did anything else, I had to immediately get my wife and my young children out of the ghetto and bring them to the courtyard where I was working. I looked around and found a place where we could all hide for a couple of days until we found some kind of solution. In this same courtyard, my brother-in-law had previously owned a large stockroom where he stored books from his publishing company, and it was our good fortune that the new owners had not yet moved these books. The stockroom doors were closed with just a latch, and it was this stockroom, behind the books, where I decided to hide my wife and children.

Incidentally, this stockroom, which stored school books and reading books from Bastomski's publishing company the Di Naye Yidishe Folkshul (New Yiddish Elementary School), was a truly important source for the children who studied in the elementary school in the ghetto until murderous hands appropriated the books. Slowly over time, Jews hid these books, saving them from being harmed by sneaking them into the ghetto, hidden under their clothes when they returned from work.[7]

As we were deemed forsaken and thus left in God's hands, my sister-in-law Malke Haymson-Bastomski—the previously mentioned and well-known teacher of the Vilna Real Gymnasium and the co-creator of the schoolbooks together with her husband Shloyme—suggested that we should leave our children with her. She had already been assured by the Judenrat that as a supervisor of the ghetto school, she would receive a yellow pass.[8] At that moment, this was the only sure possibility of saving our children, at least for now, while both our fates were hanging in the balance. My older daughter was very close to her, and she agreed to stay. However, the younger one Taybele, who was five years old at the time, could in no way be persuaded to remain with her aunt. It was extremely difficult to leave the ghetto with a child, so we had to find a sure way.

Two days prior to the great slaughter—the Yellow Pass *Aktion*[9]—we succeeded in leaving the ghetto. I brought them to the courtyard of my workplace where there was a cellar beneath the building. I temporarily brought them down to the cellar, and then went up to do my work. I went back down to the cellar after work, and we waited until it was dark outside before sneaking into the book stockroom.

7 For more on the fascinating story of how thousands of Yiddish books and manuscripts were rescued from destruction, see David E. Fishman, *The Book Smugglers: Partisans, Poets, and the Race to Save Jewish Treasures* (Lebanon, NH: ForeEdge, 2017).

8 As mentioned previously, a person with a yellow pass could save an additional three people in their family—a spouse and two children. Many who received the passes were unmarried with no children. Immediately, the process of "composing" fictitious families began in the ghetto, and every holder of a pass added people to his or her family to total four individuals. Malke Haymson-Bastomski's plan was to save the two girls by claiming that they were her daughters.

9 The Yellow Pass *Aktion* occurred over a period of two weeks between October 24, 1941, and November 5, 1941. Over 7,000 Vilna Jews were murdered during this *Aktion*. For more on this *Aktion*, see Yitzhak Arad, *Ghetto in Flames: The Struggle and Destruction of the Jews in Vilna in the Holocaust* (Jerusalem: Yad Vashem, 1980).

We lay there in the stockroom, hidden behind a mountain of scattered books. My head was splitting from trying to plan where to go and what to do next. It must have been late at night when suddenly, we heard a car enter the courtyard near the stockroom where we were lying. It came to a stop. Shortly after, we heard quiet murmuring and people moving about before hearing the sound of the car driving away.

Before it was light outside, I slipped out of the stockroom and went to the cellar to wait for the workers to arrive from the ghetto, so I could go to work together with them. It was dark in the large cellar, and it was not until I started walking around that I found myself bumping into people who were lying stretched out on the ground.

Sergeant Anton Schmid

Later that day, I solved the mystery of the departing car. I found out that the people in the car were actually escapees from the ghetto, fleeing to the town of Woronów. However, there was not always enough room in the car for all the people who were trying to leave, so they would be left behind to wait until the next night to go with another group. It wasn't until I went up to work that a friend of mine trusted me with the secret: My boss, Sergeant Anton Schmid,[10] was the one transporting Jews to Woronów every night.

10 Anton Schmid (1900–1942) was not a German but rather an Austrian electrician from Vienna who had been drafted into the German army after the 1938 *Anschluss*, which saw the annexation of Germany and Austria by Adolf Hitler. In the fall of 1941, Schmid was stationed in Vilna, where he witnessed the herding of Jews into the ghetto and the shooting of thousands of them in nearby Ponary. He saved 250 Jewish men, women, and children by providing them with forged papers and arranging their escape from Vilna to the nearby town of Woronów. In January 1942, Schmid was arrested by the Germans, tried, and sentenced to death in a military court, and on April 13, 1942, he was executed and buried in the Vilna cemetery. On October 13, 1964, Yad Vashem recognized Anton Schmid as a Righteous Among the Nations, honoring those non-Jews who risked their lives to aid and save Jews during the Holocaust. His last words in a letter to his family were as follows: "You know I have a soft heart. I couldn't think it over. I helped them, which was very bad, according to my judges. It will be hard for you…but forgive me: I acted as a human being and didn't want to hurt anyone."

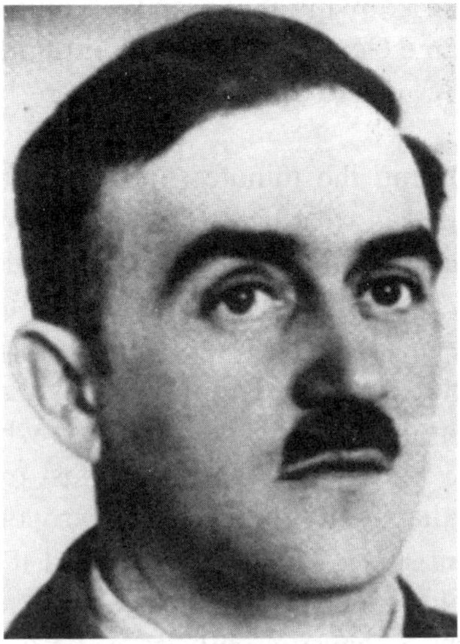

Sergeant Anton Schmid.
Photo Collection, YVA, 4613/1163.

As soon as I heard this, I sensed that a ray of salvation had suddenly appeared for us. I wanted to inform my wife about this news immediately, but I couldn't go into the stockroom now as there were Germans wandering around in the courtyard. I had to wait until evening. However, when I started work, I couldn't handle anything because my hands felt as if they were paralyzed. I waited for my boss Schmid to arrive, hanging around his office and keeping an eye out for him. It wasn't until the afternoon that I saw him enter his office alone. I quickly went over to him and said that I had something to ask him. He told me to come into his office. I did not even introduce myself before quickly making my request. Without any discussion, he told me to be ready that night at one o'clock and to wait in the cellar until he arrived with his vehicle.

I sent a letter via an acquaintance to my sister-in-law, telling her about Sergeant Schmid and our upcoming sudden departure to Woronów. Everything happened so unexpectedly! We were focused so exclusively on finding some way—any way—to get out of our desperate situation that we never even gave a single thought to where we were being taken, not even knowing if Woronów would be any different to Vilna. Weren't the same Germans there? In our minds, as long as people were allowing this German to transport them there, why should we give it any thought?

We were counting the minutes until nightfall. As soon as we heard the sound of the car, we quickly left the stockroom. A large group of people was already waiting by the vehicle. Everyone was pushing and hanging on with all their strength to get inside first, for fear of being left outside. We managed to get in the vehicle. In just a few minutes, the car was completely packed. People were lying one on top of the other. One could hear choked groans from those who were lying at the bottom. The vehicle was moving extremely fast over the poor roads, and it seemed to us that at any moment, the car would overturn. There was absolutely no air in the closed vehicle, and it was a miracle that nobody suffocated along the way.

Late that night, exhausted both from the car ride and fear, we arrived in Woronów. It was a small town where approximately 3,000 Jews had lived before the war, working in agriculture, small business, and various trades.[11] The car came to a stop at one of the first Jewish houses at the entrance to the town. Even though it was the middle of the night, all the men of the house were still awake. In order not to arouse any suspicion on the part of the town police, the men immediately began to divide us into groups of two or three to be distributed among the nearby Jewish houses.

The hospitality of the Woronów Jews was truly moving. No one refused to take as many people as they could accommodate into their homes, offering a place to sleep. They did not worry about the fact that

11 Woronów (Voranava, Voronovo) is a small town approximately 65 kilometers south of Vilna. Today, it is part of Belarus, and before World War II, it was part of Poland. In 1939, it came under the control of the Soviet Union after the Soviet occupation of Eastern Poland. The Nazis occupied the town during their invasion of Russia in June 1941. Regarding the number of Jews living in Woronów at the outbreak of World War II, about 1,000 Jews lived there, constituting the majority of its population. In January 1942, Jews from several surrounding towns were brought to the ghetto in Woronów, increasing the number of ghetto inhabitants to approximately 3,000.

it was a huge risk to harbor alien Jews, especially when we soon found out that the White-Russian police in the town were already suspicious of the newly arrived Jewish strangers.

We were taken in by a respectable Jewish family who earned a living in farming. They gave us one of the rooms in their modest-sized house and tried as much as possible to make us feel at home. On that first day, we were stunned to see how Jewish life went on in Woronów. In comparison to the hell in Vilna from which we had just fled, we felt like we had been transported to another world.

Woronów

There was no ghetto in Woronów, and all the Jews were still living in their own homes.[12] Here, the market price for food—bread, milk, and meat—was extremely cheap in comparison to the sky-high prices that just yesterday we had paid in the Vilna ghetto. This all made an enormous impression on us in those first few hours in Woronów.

We could not believe that we were only 60 kilometers from Vilna—what a difference. In Vilna, there were Nazi murderers, death, and devastation, and here, it felt like a Garden of Eden, as if there were no Germans here at all. So, we talked among ourselves: Oh, had we known about this place sooner while we were in the Vilna ghetto, we would have fled here on foot. We had no inkling of the evil that was about to befall the Vilna Jews who had escaped here.

While there were only a few dozen German soldiers here in the town, in coordination with the fascist White-Russian police, they caused much misery for the Woronów Jews. They forced the Jews to work, they beat them, and they extorted money from them. But mass murders were not yet known here.

Every night, Sergeant Schmid, who had brought us here, would bring new groups in his car, and within a few days, there were already

12 In fact, there was a ghetto in Woronów at this time, but unlike the Vilna ghetto from where Lazar had just arrived, the Jews were still living in their own homes.

more than 300 Vilna Jews in Woronów. We decided to bring our older daughter Malkele, whom we had left in the ghetto with our sister-in-law. The following night, I waited for Schmid and his car in order to go back with him and bring her to Woronów together with my sister-in-law, if she chose to come along. This was November 1, 1941. Schmid did not come that night nor the next night. We understood that something must have happened, and the plan to bring our little daughter to Woronów came to naught. Refugees from Vilna later brought us the tragic news of the dreadful slaughter that became known as the Yellow Pass *Aktion*.

The 300 Vilna Jews living in Woronów soon caught the attention of both the Germans in the town and the White-Russian police. Indeed, a few days later, the Judenrat received an order that all alien Jews who had entered the town must register with the local *gmina*.[13] This was the first indication of lurking danger for the escaped Vilna Jews. The owner of the house where we were staying also believed this and advised us not to wait and to look for a way to flee to Lida, just 32 kilometers from Woronów. Lida, he said, is a larger city with almost 7,000 Jews, and therefore, strangers would not stand out as much to the local authorities.

This was truly good advice. Right away, he took me to a peasant whom he knew to discuss the matter. At first, the peasant hesitated, expressing his fear of traveling with Jews. We told him that we would remove the yellow patches from our clothing as soon as we left town, and when we offered him a fine sum of money for his trouble, he consented. We arranged to leave early on Sunday morning, when the police would be sleeping off a night of drinking.

This was on Friday, November 14, 1941. At around ten in the morning, I went to a house on a nearby street to see some Vilna acquaintances who were staying there and to find out what people were saying about the registration and whether anyone had already registered. As we were sitting there, each worried about the ominous hour that was approaching us Vilnaites, the owner of the house entered, deadly pale, with fear in his eyes. He gave us the news that the police were forcing everyone into their houses, warning that anyone who was found in the

13 The Polish word *gmina* is best translated as township. A *gmina* was the smallest Polish territorial unit of administration.

street would be shot. After hearing this news, it was clear to us that they were preparing for action against the Jews. We all sat there frightened and confused, like condemned people.

"What should I do? How do I reach my wife and child now?" I said in desperation. "At such a moment after all, I need to be with them."

The owner of the house warned me not to go, telling me it would be certain death and maybe we would get away with just a scare. Turning to me again, he said that since I was not part of the household, it would be better for now if I went into the stable and hid there under the hay. That is what I did. I lay there under the hay until evening, peering out impatiently, waiting for someone from the house to come and tell me what was happening. The owner of the house finally arrived. He told me to crawl out from under the hay, and then he quietly told me what had happened.

The White-Russian police and the Germans had gone from house to house, gathering all the alien Jews who had recently arrived in town. They were taken to the movie theater building, and no one knew what would happen to them. They had not bothered any of the town's Jews. With this, he informed me that I must leave the stable immediately because the Germans had announced that they would be searching all the houses again, and wherever they found an alien Jew, the entire family would be shot.

Upon hearing this terrible news, I started to weep hysterically. The man attempted to console me, saying that the imprisoned Jews would probably be sent to work like the town's Jews and that they would most likely be released afterward. My heart, however, told me that this was going to be bad.

I asked him for advice as to what I should do and where I should go now. I started to try and persuade him to let me spend one more night in the stable, suggesting that he should not lock the door. If the police caught me, it would appear as if I had entered the stable and was hiding there without his knowledge. Seeing my desperation, he didn't have the heart to refuse, and he told me to bury myself even deeper under the hay. That night stretched on and on. It felt like a year. My teeth were chattering. I could barely wait until morning when I would be able to find out about the fate of the arrestees.

At dawn, without being noticed, I left the stable and sneaked back to the house where I had been with my wife and child. When the owners of the house saw me, they burst into tears and told me that my wife and child, my Taybele, had been taken away. They also warned that it was dangerous both for me and for them if I were to remain there for even one more minute and that the best thing for me to do would be to disappear from town that day, as they would certainly be searching every house for Vilna Jews in hiding. They advised me to go to Lida on foot.

But now the question was this: How can I leave when the town is surrounded by police? I convinced the owners of the house to allow me to hide in the stable under the hay until nightfall. Then they would show me a side road leading out of town. They promised to do whatever they could to help release my wife and child from the police. They even said they would use their own money if it would help.

Late that night, the house owner called me down from the loft and, unnoticed by anyone, he led me through a field to the other side of town, cautioning me to go only through fields and forests until I reached Lida. For that whole night, the entire following day, and then again another night, I wandered through muddy fields and forests with nothing to eat because I was afraid to approach a peasant's house to ask for food lest I encountered the local police.

Early in the morning, with my last ounce of strength, hungry and totally exhausted, I arrived in Lida. Before the war, Lida was a city with a population of 30,000 inhabitants, among them 13,000 Jews. It had a flourishing Jewish cultural community life. Now, the entire city center lay in ruins. Of the 13,000 Jews, only 7,000 were still alive.[14] It was my good fortune to meet a Jew on the street who, seeing that I was not wearing a yellow patch—an offense for which in Lida one would be immediately shot—took me right away into his house. Once inside the

14 At the outbreak of World War II, there were, in fact, 6,300 Jews in Lida, comprising about one-third of its total population. However, when World War II began in September 1939, Lida was occupied by the Soviets. Due to an influx of Jewish refugees fleeing from the German-occupied areas of Poland, the Jewish population in Lida increased to approximately 7,000 and continued to grow in the following months.

house, I told him about my entire tragic experience and asked for his advice as to what I should do here and to whom I should turn.

From One Hell to Another

When I arrived in Lida, the ghetto had not yet been established.[15] Since the Jew who had taken me in that morning could not do much to help me, he suggested that I turn to one of the representatives of the Judenrat,[16] and he gave me an address. After he had provided me with the yellow patches for both the front and the back of my clothes, as required by law, I set out to visit the Judenrat member at the given address.

His name was Ilutovitch. Even before the war, he had been a respected community activist in Lida. It turned out that this Ilutovitch had a son-in-law named Levinson, who was a doctor. They lived together in the same house, and this doctor actually remembered me from his time at Vilna University. He was a frequent visitor at the *Vilner Tog* newspaper, where I worked as a compositor. I had gotten very lucky: After all, in a strange city, one feels more comfortable among acquaintances, especially in such times and under such circumstances.

They welcomed me as if I was one of their own, and after telling them about my entire tragic experience in Woronów, they calmed me down and assured me that they would do everything that was necessary to help me. Before anything else, I had to be registered as a local resident, but in the meantime, I stayed with them. However, to me, my life no longer mattered. Despite how good these friendly people were to

15 In December 1941, the Lida Jews were forced to leave their homes and move into the ghetto. The Lida ghetto was sealed later that month.

16 The first Judenrat in Lida consisted of fourteen members and was headed by Kalman Lichtman, a teacher from the Jewish high school. The other senior members included entrepreneur Simcha Kotok and lawyers Israel Kreczner and Benjamin Cederowicz. See "Lida," in Geoffrey P. Megargee, ed., *The United States Holocaust Memorial Museum Encyclopedia of Camps and Ghettos, 1933–1945, vol. 2: Ghettos in German-Occupied Eastern Europe* (Bloomington: Indiana University Press, 2012), p. 1226.

me, my wife and child were in the hands of the murderers, and I could not save them. The sparse information that was arriving from Woronów deprived me of any hope that I would ever see them again.

Due to the tragic events in Woronów, the stream of escaped Vilna Jews began to flow into Lida. Within a short time, Lida had almost 1,000 refugees from Vilna. Both the fatalities in Woronów and the fear that the same thing might one day be repeated here motivated me to become a true Lida citizen. It just so happened that at this time, the township administration was distributing passes to the Lida residents. Since the city had been almost entirely burned down[17] and the previous official records no longer existed, it was only necessary to specify a burned-out house and allege that this was where you had previously lived. In addition, the Judenrat had bribed a couple of Polish clerks from the department responsible for the distribution of passes—anyone who suspected that something was not quite right had to be bribed. In this way, all the refugees from Vilna received passes and became legal Lida residents.

It is worth mentioning here that the first Lida Judenrat was of great assistance to the Vilna refugees in establishing their citizenship, even paying for those who did not have enough money to cover the cost of the pass. For this help, the members of the Judenrat paid with their lives when a Jewish traitor informed on them to the German authorities.

In the ghetto, I secured a small spot in a room with seven other people. Compared to the living conditions in the Vilna ghetto, where twenty-three people had lived in a similar-sized room, one could consider it quite comfortable. However, while everyone was preoccupied with settling into their little corner of a room so as to somehow get by in the ghetto, hoping to survive until the liberation, for me the sad days continued to pass by. I would walk around in a daze, constantly inquiring if anyone had heard anything about Woronów.

Two weeks later, a group of Jews who worked outside the ghetto met a peasant from Woronów who told them about the tragic end of the Vilna refugees who had been gathered together and imprisoned in the local movie theater. And so, there was no doubt that the fate of my

17 During the occupation of Lida by the Germans on June 27, 1941, the city suffered heavy bombing and shelling.

wife and my young, little daughter was sealed: They perished as Jewish martyrs in Woronów, even before our nearest ones in Vilna were sent to Ponary. They had already finished suffering the hell of this world. However, my cup of anguish was apparently not yet full. Fate had it that my wife perished on our tenth wedding anniversary. I remember on that day ten years earlier, there had been a pogrom against the Jews of Vilna after the student activist Vatslovski had been killed. It was difficult to reconcile myself to the idea that my wife and child were no longer among the living. But the knowledge that my older daughter Malkele was still in Vilna gave me strength, and little by little, I began to adapt to my new life in the ghetto.

The order for forced labor—for men aged fourteen to sixty and for women aged sixteen to forty—was strictly enforced here. Since I had worked on the train lines in Vilna, I asked the Judenrat to assign me to the train lines here. At the time, I did not realize that I was bringing trouble upon myself. I was initially assigned the job of unloading cars of coal. Three men working with shovels had to empty a car within a period of two hours. Performing this work demanded all our strength, and we also turned black from the coal dust that even reached our underwear.

At first, I thought that this was the worst job one could do, but very soon, I was convinced that this was actually a "good" job. One time, they needed someone to work in the depot where the locomotives were repaired, and it was me who had the bad luck to get chosen. The depot boss, a fat German with a gluttonous mug, was a monster. I was assigned the task of cleaning the locomotives. For ten hours every day, I had to lie underneath the locomotives and use rags to clean every single part of the locomotive with the greatest German precision. After such a day of work, I was barely able to straighten my back, and I barely had the strength to drag myself back to the ghetto 4 kilometers away.

But that wasn't all. I was often covered in grease, which was even worse than the coal dust. The oil would drip from the locomotives and completely soak through my clothes. After work like this, what was needed was a hot, soapy bath, and that was something I could only dream about. In the ghetto, there were no baths, and outside the ghetto, baths were off-limits.

We had half an hour for lunch. We were given half a liter of "soup" made from some kind of flour. It was bitter like bile. However, I had no other choice, so I ate it. I had no other food, but at least this hot "soup" warmed me up during the extremely cold weather. I cursed my life and cried over my bitter fate. Day and night, all I thought about was how I could stop doing this accursed work. I did not dare walk away from the work on my own accord or even to change my workplace—that, most likely, would have been the end of me. Not coming to work was permitted only if you had a fever higher than 38 degrees Celsius (100.4 degrees Fahrenheit) and could provide a certificate from a doctor in the Judenrat infirmary. But even in such a case, the doctors were reluctant to issue such a certificate for fear of checks, which took place quite often.

Death also threatened those who were late for work, even by just a few minutes. Many people had already paid with their lives for just such an offense, and during my time working on the train lines, such tragic cases actually occurred. There was one time when ten Jews were late by just a few minutes. They were extremely fortunate in getting away with just twenty-five lashes to their naked bodies.

A second case ended very tragically, however. Fifteen men were late by fifteen minutes. The bloodthirsty train boss immediately telephoned headquarters to report the incident. A German police division arrived and led the unfortunate ones a short distance away from where they had been standing. A few minutes later, a volley of bullets ended their lives.

Another incident involved eleven Jews who did not come to their regular work because, on that day, they were working at a different place. They had even received permits for this other work. But this did not help them to avoid death. The Judenrat received an order from the police to immediately send these eleven men to their original workplace. A short time later, their bodies were found riddled with murderous bullets. On orders from the police, the Judenrat later removed the corpses and buried them in the cemetery near the ghetto.

CHAPTER TWO

SURVIVAL IN LIDA

In the Lida Ghetto

In general, the situation for the Jews in the Lida ghetto was different from that in the Vilna ghetto, because mass slaughters, such as those conducted by the Nazis in Vilna as well as in the rest of Lithuania at that time, had not yet occurred in Lida. There was one exception, which occurred immediately after the occupation of Lida, when the Nazis shot 150 out of a group of 300 captured Jews and then released the others, allowing them to go home. Here, the devil followed our every step, both at work and on our way to work. For every minor infraction, we were exposed to death. If a Jew "sinned" and was shot, his entire family was removed from the ghetto to share the same fate.

Jews received 100 grams of bitter black bread per person per day in the ghetto, and twice a day, soup—a thin liquid in which one would rarely find a few grains or pieces of potato—was distributed. It was forbidden to buy something from a Christian outside the ghetto. But what does one do when hunger persists? And not so much for oneself as for one's children, who, after all, did not understand anything and pleaded for food. People would ignore the danger to their lives and risk buying any kind of food from the local population, smuggling it into the ghetto upon their return from work. The White-Russian police, however, lurked everywhere, ready to nab Jews who were committing such offenses. They hid between the walls of the burned-out houses and waited there to catch a person who was smuggling something into the ghetto. So, there were victims just about every day.

One day, a stroke of luck freed me from my dreadful work at the train depot. While at work, a heavy piece of iron fell on my hand, and the sharp edge of the iron chopped off part of my finger. Although at that moment I was experiencing unbearable pain and the blood was gushing freely, in my heart I was happy that this had occurred, thinking that perhaps now I would be released from my loathsome work. And, indeed, that is what actually happened.

It took a couple of weeks for my finger to heal somewhat before the Judenrat sent me off to work again. But because of my injured finger, I did not return to the accursed train depot. This time, I was assigned to work at the German police headquarters, right in the midst of the murderers themselves, who already had many butchered Jewish lives on their consciences. More than thirty Jews worked there doing various jobs. At the time, I was very scared to be in this new place. To be in the hands of the murderers and to see their murderous faces all day long—this alone terrified me. But I had no choice.

I was assigned to a group that sawed and chopped the wood needed to heat the ovens. The work itself was bearable, but one had to be extremely careful when taking a brief rest. Our immediate supervisor was a policeman named Sobolewski. Besides being a horrible murderer, he was also a neurotic and severe drunkard. Whenever we saw him approaching, we were overcome with fear. The older policeman—a higher-ranking guard—was a tall, fat German who, when he was drunk, was a danger to the Jews who worked there and encountered him. We had to watch out for him as if he was the Angel of Death. Even his own policemen feared him. These two loathsome characters were our bosses, and their bullying of the Jewish workers, who did the most strenuous work for them, had no restraint nor limit. When we arrived at work early each morning, it was not certain that we would return to the ghetto later that day.

Lunchtime was between twelve and one o'clock. The kitchen that was used to feed the Jews was located outside the ghetto and continued to exist until shortly before the liquidation. The female kitchen manager was a depraved antisemite, and the provision of food for the Jews in the ghetto was in this woman's hands. At the beginning, we all went to the kitchen together in a group to get our portion of soup. However, since the lines were very long at lunchtime, we did not always have enough time to get to the window where the soup was being dispensed. We would then have to run back to work—still hungry—in order to not be late to get back to work promptly at one o'clock. So instead, we found a pail, and two men would go to the kitchen every day to collect everyone's portion of soup.

One day, the two men brought back the soup precisely at one o'clock, when the lunch hour had ended. We were hungry and freezing. Everyone yearned for a little hot soup to warm their frozen limbs. We deliberated and decided to ask the policeman Sobolewski for permission to have five minutes to eat our lunch. For this insolence, he began to beat the guy who had come to him with the request. We started work right away, scared for our lives and having not eaten.

When the policeman left, two men who could not resist the temptation went over to the pail and took some soup with their tin dipper. At that exact moment, we heard three shots, and in the blink of an eye, that same policeman came running toward us, gun in hand and in a fiery rage, ordering us to undress immediately. We all turned white. I thought that this was the end for me. For several seconds that seemed to stretch out for an eternity, we stood there frozen with apprehension. Then, he shouted: "You will work into the night, wearing just your underwear. The next time, you will be shot for not obeying my orders." We breathed freely again. Only then did we feel the bitter frost that was cutting into our naked skin like a knife.

The regional commissar in charge of Lida and the surrounding region was a young German named Hermann Hanweg.[18] This young

18 Hermann Hanweg was the German *Gebietskommissar* (regional commissar) in

Nazi was the real boss in control of the lives and possessions of the thousands of Jews in Lida as well as all the other towns in the region. He surrounded himself with a retinue of sadists and mistresses whom he had brought over from Germany. They settled themselves into the best houses that had been undamaged by the fire.

From his very first day in Lida, he began to extract valuable assets from the Jews in a well-thought-out way to send back home to Germany. He would summon the chairman of the Judenrat and hand him lists of expensive furs, jewelry, sets of tableware, gold, and other valuable objects—and he demanded them immediately! Collecting all these items from among the Lida Jews was no easy job for the Judenrat. They would carry this Jewish property to the Nazi commissar with bitter hearts but with the hope that in exchange for the price of these valuables, the day of the final decree might be deferred a little longer. But as soon as Hanweg and his retinue had been satiated with the Jewish possessions, the grim destruction, the horrors, and the slaughters began in Lida, just like in every other place where the Hitlerist hordes rampaged.

For the Jews in the ghetto, there were no days off work. Hanweg found jobs for us, even on Sundays when we were free from our daily forced labor in the various German military units. An order was issued to the Judenrat: Jews had to work on Sundays, dismantling the ruins of the burned-out houses and cleaning up the area. A group of Polish employees from the city council supervised this work, and the White-Russian police made sure that everyone worked diligently, giving these bosses an opportunity to harass the Jews and extort money and other

Lida. His deputy was Leopold Windisch. Hanweg joined the Nazi party in 1928. He was captured by the Russians at the end of the war and shot as a war criminal in 1946. Historian Wendy Lower writes the following in her book about him: "In Lida, the Hanweg children attended a special German school and played in the local parks and forests. They routinely accompanied their mother and father on tours of the ghetto workshops, where thousands of Jews tried desperately to stay alive by fulfilling every order and whim of the local Germans. To please the commissar, a team of Jewish craftsmen created an elaborate electric train set for his son's birthday. They also presented Hanweg with a set of rings, one for each member of the family." See Wendy Lower, *Hitler's Furies: German Women in the Nazi Killing Fields* (New York: Houghton Mifflin Harcourt, 2013), p. 101.

valuable items from them. It was much harder to bear the suffering from these local hooligans than from the Germans. The pain in our hearts was even greater because, after all, they were local Poles who until recently had been our neighbors.

Within the regional commissar's entourage was a certain German by the name of Rudolf Werner,[19] an underworld type and a sadist. He looked like Hermann Göring,[20] with the exact same build and large belly. This Werner had a dog with whom he never parted. Werner's great delight was to sit on a comfortable stool on the balcony of the house in the area where the Jews worked in the ruins on Sundays and to send down his dog, inciting him to set upon the working Jews. The dog would throw himself upon someone, tear his clothes, and often tear off pieces of flesh with his sharp teeth. The unfortunate one would struggle with the dog in great desperation, while at the same time, this contemptible lowlife would burst into laughter at this game. Once, the dog was sick, and this madman notified the Judenrat that if the dog died, ten Jews would be shot. To their good fortune, the dog did not die, and the Jews got away with just a scare.

19 Rudolf Werner was the *Gebietskommissar* in Baranowicze (Baranavichy). After the war, he was on the run for many years. Finally, he was arrested in 1964 in the city of Mainz, Germany, where his trial also took place. He is remembered by survivors as being almost 2 meters tall and an athletic type. His trial ended without punishment. Historian Christian Gerlach cites the testimony of Werner's interpreter in the legal proceedings against him in the 1960s in Munich. According to this testimony, Werner was an "enthusiastic supporter of the extermination of the Jews" and claimed that "Jews are enemies of the German people and have no right to exist in the German Reich." See Christian Gerlach, *Kalkulierte Morde: Die Deutsche Wirtschafts- und Vernichtungspolitik in Weissrussland 1941 bis 1944* (Hamburg: Hamburger Edition, 1999), p. 702.

20 Hermann Göring (1893–1946) was a prominent figure in Nazi Germany. He served as a World War I fighter pilot and later became a key figure in the Nazi Party, earning significant influence under Adolf Hitler's regime. He held various high-ranking positions within the Nazi government, including the role of Hitler's designated successor, and he was one of the primary architects of the Holocaust. Göring was condemned to hang as a war criminal by the International Military Tribunal at Nürnberg (Nuremberg) in 1946, but he committed suicide by poisoning himself instead.

Five Hundred Rabbit Chasers

One Sunday,[21] Hanweg issued an order to the Judenrat to provide 500 Jewish men to meet in the courtyard at seven o'clock in the morning. For what purpose did he need 500 Jewish men? Fear enveloped the ghetto. But an order is an order. The Jewish police were given the task of rounding up the specified number of men. Everyone was hiding wherever they could. But there was no way to avoid it, and at the appointed time, the Jewish police provided the requested 500 Jews. It was my fate to be included in this group.

That day, there was a terrible frost. At seven in the morning, all 500 men were standing in the courtyard, our teeth chattering from both the cold and fear. Soon, the forest guards arrived with rifles slung over their shoulders, and we learned from them that a rabbit hunt had been organized. The entire retinue of Nazis would be participating, with the regional commissar at the front. They needed us as rabbit chasers. Our hearts lightened a little. "So, we will be rabbit chasers," we muttered to each other. As long as we were not being led to our death.

The Jews in the ghetto no longer had any warm clothes. In Lida, as in all the other ghettos, the Jews had been forced to give up their furs to the Nazi rulers. Not only were Jews not allowed to wear any furs but they also could not have fur collars on their coats or own fur gloves. For hiding furs, a Jew risked death.

At eight o'clock, we began to move. The forest guards brought us to a field 4 kilometers from Lida and ordered us to remain standing there until the hunters—the important dignitaries—arrived. Standing in the deep snow and waiting was a great hardship for us. We were dressed in thin clothes, and our shoes were torn. Some did not even have shoes and had wrapped their feet in rags. We stood there like that, shivering

21 As mentioned, Sundays were days off from forced labor, however German soldiers or police would often take Jews then for unpaid work. On the incident of the rabbit chasers mentioned here, see also the testimony of Shmuel Amarant in Alexander Manor, Yitzhak Ganuzovitz, and Aba Lando, eds., *Sefer Lida* (Hebrew) (Tel Aviv: Irgun Yotzei Lida BeYisrael Uva'ad Ha'ezra Liyehudey Lida BeArtzot Habrit, 1970).

from the cold. Some people's fingers and toes were already beginning to freeze.

At eleven o'clock, the entire group arrived with their wives and loved ones. They were all dressed in furs and warm hats, with bolsters on their feet, all of which, not so long ago, had belonged to the very same Jews who were standing there. The Jewish furriers must have altered these things for them. We were ordered to form a circle. The entire group of Nazis stood in the center, and one of them called out to us.

"Jews, the entire success of the rabbit hunt depends on the chasers. Therefore, you must exactly follow all the instructions I am giving you here. All the chasers have to be in one line, spread out, with five steps separating one from the next, and when the rabbits begin to run, you have to shout loudly at the top of your voice. Anyone who does not obey this order will be shot."

We started running through the forests, which were covered in deep snow that reached our knees. After two hours of nonstop running, we had no strength left, but we had warmed up. The sweat poured from us and soaked us through and through. Suddenly, an order was issued to stop and form a circle once again. The same German informed us that the hunt was not going well, and he warned us again to carry out his orders correctly.

After a short time, the entire group of hunters left, and we thought that the German's warning had just been an idle threat and that the rabbit hunt had ended. But then, to our surprise, a sled arrived carrying bread. The forest guards told us that we would be receiving some portions of bread and that the hunt would resume when the hunters returned from lunch. At the end of the hunt, totally exhausted and with our last bit of strength, we dragged ourselves back to the ghetto in the middle of the night. With no time to recover, we had to run to work once again.

The Tragic End of the First Lida Judenrat

It was the beginning of March 1942. One night, thieves broke into the home of a White-Russian priest who lived near the ghetto. The priest woke up in time to nab one of the thieves, but the thief was stronger than the priest, so he beat him up and fled. In the morning, the priest notified the German police, and they came to question him about the nighttime attack. The battered priest told the police that the thieves were Jews and that he would recognize them if they were caught.

That same day, Hanweg ordered the chairman of the Judenrat Kalman Lichtman to immediately bring all the ghetto thieves to the police headquarters, saying that if this was not done, innocent Jews would suffer.[22] Indeed, there were several thieves in the ghetto, who caused much distress by robbing houses, and the Judenrat was unable to deal with them effectively. But, no one knew for sure if it was actually these ghetto thieves who had attacked the priest.

The Judenrat had no other choice but to give up these criminals, whose loathsome acts might have resulted in the death of everyone in the ghetto. The Jewish police were successful in apprehending only a few of the thieves. The rest of them had managed to get away and had disappeared somewhere. Those who were caught, however, were brought to the police headquarters in the morning as required by the order.

One of the arrested criminals, whose name was Virobek, betrayed the Judenrat by informing on them.[23] During the investigation, he proposed to the police that if they let him live, he would give them very important information regarding the Judenrat. Then, he told them how the Judenrat had prepared false passes for the Vilna refugees. That same day, the German police arrested all the members of the Judenrat and carried out searches in their homes as well as in the Judenrat offices.

22 According to our knowledge, in early March 1942, it was Leopold Windisch—responsible for Jewish affairs within the civil administration in Lida—who discovered that Jews from the ghetto were accused of robbing an Orthodox priest. He demanded that the Judenrat, headed by Kalman Lichtman, hand over the thieves. The Judenrat surrendered four men who, in turn, revealed that a number of Jews had escaped from the massacres in Vilna and had found refuge in Lida at the end of 1941.

23 The person who supposedly informed on the Vilna Jews in the Lida ghetto was Yankel Avidon. He managed to flee to Vilna, where he was arrested, put on trial, and sentenced to death by the Jewish ghetto court. See Einat, *Hayei Yom-Yom Begeto Vilna*, pp. 152–153.

Their first action was to take all the money belonging to the Judenrat that had been collected from the taxes paid by each person for his little bit of living space in the ghetto, which the Judenrat would use for various purposes.

The entire ghetto was agitated. Nobody could figure out why they had been arrested. Various rumors circled the ghetto, but nobody knew the truth. For two weeks, the police conducted investigations. The unfortunate members of the Judenrat suffered unbearable torture, but they did not admit anything. The Gestapo men, led by the regional commissar, then devised a sophisticated plan to identify those Vilna refugees who had received false passes: they would use Virobek to identify them.

It is important to note that the Lida Jews were confined in three separate ghettos in different parts of the town. This was because the occupiers could not find enough houses for all 7,000 Jews within one section of the burned-out city. One of the ghettos was located on Kosharowa Street, a second on Postawska Street, and the third in the Piaski district.[24] Until the horrific slaughter that occurred later on May 8, 1942, the Judenrat offices were located on Kosharowa Street. Later, after the slaughter, only around 1,300 of the over 7,000 Jews survived, and the only remaining ghetto was located on Postawska Street until its liquidation.

On the morning of *Erev* Purim,[25] as we were waking up and quickly getting ready for work like we did every day, we saw large groups of armed Lithuanian police in their yellow uniforms and White-Russian police under the command of the Germans entering the ghetto. They spread out across the ghetto streets, driving everyone out of their

24 The Lida ghetto was established in three separate quarters of the town. The most important section was on Postawska and Chłodna Streets, including the Jewish cemetery; the second section was on Kosharowa Street and Gastello Street, close to the forest of Borowka; and the third was in the Piaski district between the streets Jalowa, Zurawlinaja, and Orlicz-Dreszer. This section had been predominantly Christian before and therefore had to be cleared for this purpose. Houses on both sides of Postawska Street near the river were surrounded by barbed wire. See "Lida," in Megargee, *Encyclopedia of Camps and Ghettos, vol. 2*, p. 1226.

25 In 1942, *Erev* (the eve of) Purim was on March 2.

houses with wild shouts of "Get out!" They did not even give us time to get dressed. Anyone who didn't have enough time to throw on a piece of outer clothing had to run out of the house in their underwear. Elderly people, who were sick and weak and unable to get up from their beds, were shot by the beasts as they lay there.

In the house where I was staying, there was a young couple, and the woman had just given birth the day before. This was actually forbidden according to the Nazi ghetto laws. She was still very weak, so her husband quickly threw a coat over her and, with the help of some neighbors, led her and the baby out of the house before the murderers entered. Had they not done this, she would have been shot. But they were still unable to elude death when the mass slaughter took place. Later, the woman's sister was with me in the forest, and she would constantly recall their tragic fate.

Under a hail of blows, the thugs drove us toward the ghetto gate. The only thought in each person's mind was that this was the end, the final road leading to death. Those who were able made their way over to the barbed-wire fence that surrounded the ghetto to somehow force themselves through to the other side and hide from death. But every escapee who was spotted by the brutes was immediately shot on the spot. In the first few minutes, tens of people were murdered in this way.

Together with another Jew, I successfully climbed over the ghetto fence at a point near the workshops located outside the ghetto, where several hundred Jews worked doing various jobs for the German army. We ducked into a warehouse where there was a deep pit, inside of which lay a large metal barrel with pipes extending outward. Since we were worried that the Nazis would come in search of those who were hiding, we both crawled into the pit and hid behind the barrel. However, there was only room for one person, so we lay one on top of the other. Indeed, it turned out that our assumption was correct. A short time later, somebody opened the door and then quickly closed it. At the same time, we heard gunshots in the courtyard, an indication that the murderers had found hidden Jews.

We lay in the ditch the entire night, formulating various plans about where to go if the ghetto was being liquidated. My partner in misery was employed in the workshops as a tailor. He was from Lida and was familiar with the entire surrounding area. He assured me that, regardless of what might happen, we would stay together.

At daybreak, we heard Yiddish being spoken near the warehouse where we were lying. We peeked through a crack in the wall, and the tailor—I don't remember his name—immediately recognized that these were Jews who worked in the stable. We quickly left the warehouse to ask them what had happened in the ghetto. When I found out that there had not, in fact, been a slaughter, I felt that I could no longer stay there and listen to their stories. My intuition told me that I had to return to the ghetto to catch my work group before it left for work duties at the German police headquarters. If I did not get there in time to join them, I would be finished. Within just a few minutes, I had climbed back into the ghetto over the same fence through which I had escaped the day before. Luckily for me, I met the entire group in the ghetto, and I was soon on my way with them to my grueling work, without time to get a little hot water.

Confusion among the Vilna Refugees

The same horrific scenes that had occurred on Postawska Street, where I lived, were also playing out in the other two ghettos on Kosharowa Street and in the Piaski district from where everybody had been driven out to the marketplace under a hail of blows. The Jews remained standing in the marketplace for several hours until the regional commissar, the chief of the German police, and their entourage arrived. Soon, the informer Virobek was seen being led out under heavy guard. The rounded-up Jews were ordered to march, one behind the other, past the thief Virobek. He stared at each one and pointed out anyone whom he recognized as a Vilna refugee. That person was led to the side, and the line continued to move forward past this lowlife until all had filed by. While the Jews were standing in place and waiting, convinced there would be a massacre, each one tore up the money he had with him and buried it in the snow. They did the same with their watches and other valuable items. They did not want the enemies to get any benefit from these belongings.

The weather that day was bitterly cold with a biting wind. The desperate Jews had to stand there until the sad procession was over before the Germans ordered anyone remaining to return to the ghetto. The informant recognized more than thirty Vilna refugees. They were immediately taken to prison under heavy guard. As a result of this *Aktion*, the three ghettos in Lida suffered a loss of over 200 victims.

After the arrest of the Vilnaites, the investigation to find others began anew. A Jewish hairdresser from the ghetto who worked in the prison related that there were confrontations between the arrested Vilnaites and the Judenrat, and that he had heard terrible screams, however the tortured ones remained steadfast and betrayed no one. A few days later, the German police came into the ghetto and removed everything from the houses of those who had been arrested. And on that same day, the more than thirty Vilnaites together with the members of the Judenrat were shot just a few meters from the prison. Three of those condemned threw themselves to the ground just before the shots were fired. Those who were shot fell on top of them, and they remained lying underneath the mass of slain bodies.

When the Hitlerists had completed their bloody work, they went off to get drunk, leaving it to the ghetto Jews to remove the corpses and bury them. The survivors lay there late into the night in their secure hiding place underneath the bloodied bodies of their brothers who had been shot. Later, they crept out from under the heap of corpses and disappeared into the dark night. We found out about this later. I remember two of them. One, who was called Gamarski, had lived in Vilna on Lipuvka Street, and the other one, Antske Kenski, was the youngest son of a well-known Vilna flour merchant. The three survivors returned to the Vilna ghetto, where they perished during the liquidation of the ghetto on September 23–24, 1943.

After every massacre, the Judenrat would send a wagon to take the victims to the cemetery for burial. It was only then that one could see the kind of barbarous torture they had suffered prior to being shot. Heartrending scenes played out when someone recognized a loved one. In this case, the bodies of the murdered Judenrat members were black, covered with deep wounds, and with nothing more than skin and bones remaining following the torture they had withstood before their deaths.

Immediately after the slaughter, the regional commissar issued an order to form a new Judenrat. It was initially difficult to find volunteers who were willing to risk their lives for the benefit of the community, but there was no other option, and somehow a new Judenrat was assembled.[26]

A few weeks later, another tragic incident occurred. This time, they arrested more than seventy Jews who were working in a German unit called the Beuthen camp, where they would gather the loot that the German army had seized. The Germans accused the arrested Jews of stealing weapons from the camp. Even though a search turned up nothing, everyone was still taken to prison. Later, it was discovered that the Christian Poles who also worked there had made this accusation. Apparently, they were the ones who had actually stolen the weapons, either to use themselves or to sell to the partisans. In order to deflect any suspicion from themselves, they accused the Jewish workers. So now, there were over seventy new victims of the ghetto.

At the same time, information began to reach the ghetto about the slaughters that had been carried out against the Jews in the towns of White Russia. Optimists comforted the nervous population and convinced themselves and others that the regional commissar Hanweg would not permit the Lida ghetto to be annihilated, "because he needed the Jews for labor, and especially because in the ghetto workshops, important things were being manufactured that were very necessary for the soldiers on the battlefields, and therefore he would not permit his useful Jews to be murdered." In this manner, they carried on hair-splitting discussions among themselves in their homes in the evenings after they had returned from their forced labor.

To secure their safety, people in Lida began to seek various ways of somehow sneaking into "lucky" workshops to get a skilled-worker pass, similar to what had occurred in Vilna during the period of the yellow passes. The regional commissar's Jewish confidant, who was also the supervisor of the workshops and the Jewish workers, was an engineer from Galicia, an assimilated Jew by the name of Altman.[27]

26 The physician Dr. Czarny was appointed the new chairman of the Judenrat.

27 This is referring to the engineer Altman, who was a former director of the Benland foundry.

During this time, Altman exploited the situation so as to profit from the Jews' troubles. For the price of several gold tsarist ten-ruble coins (*hazerlech*),[28] he would bring someone into the workshops and issue the person with a skilled-worker pass, which would supposedly provide protection during the time of a slaughter. The ghetto dubbed these skilled workers "golden workers." In this way, Altman amassed a sizeable fortune, and he must have surely believed that Hanweg would permit him to live for the service he was rendering.

After the tragic murder of the Judenrat and the single-file procession at the marketplace, a great anxiety developed among the Vilna refugees. They were afraid that the head of the German police would employ all kinds of tactics in order to nab the Vilnaites. So, there was a panicked return to the Vilna ghetto where, at that time, the situation had somewhat stabilized.[29]

Such a trip to Vilna was not only fraught with danger at every step of the way but also expensive—one needed a lot of money to get there. Any peasant who risked transporting Jews to Vilna on his wagon through the back roads demanded an exorbitant price. As for me, I could only dream about this, but those who were able to pay and had such an opportunity did not let the danger deter them. So, one way or another, a significant number of Vilna refugees fled the Lida ghetto and returned to Vilna.

During this period, the level of anxiety in the ghetto remained high, as people were searching for both skilled-worker passes and a "secure" workplace. For now, such a pass was considered to be the only sure way to save oneself in case of a massacre. At this point, very few people in the ghetto considered an escape into the forest, because there was almost no knowledge about the existence of partisan activity. Day and night, we lived in an environment filled with anxiety and confusion.

At the beginning of May 1942, Hanweg summoned the members of the Judenrat. He issued a statement saying that information had

28 *Hazerlech* is a Yiddish word meaning little pigs and was used by the Jews to describe these coins.

29 The massive murder of the Vilna Jews ended at the close of 1941. After that, there was a relatively calm period that lasted about a year and a half. It is referred to as the "period of stability" of the Vilna ghetto.

reached him about the Jews hiding gold and valuable jewelry, which had not yet been turned over to him. He said that he was giving them three days to gather this hidden gold from the Jews and to bring it to him. He finished by saying that if this was not carried out by the deadline, he could not guarantee the outcome for this disobedience.

The Judenrat gathered all the Jews in the ghetto and related the regional commissar's words. They appealed to those who still had gold and jewelry to turn it over to the Judenrat and perhaps avert the calamity destined for the ghetto. Even though we already knew in our hearts that a massacre was unavoidable, we still held a spark of hope. Perhaps some gold would soften the regional commissar's heart, and he would call off the planned slaughter. People began to bring gold and jewelry to the Judenrat.

However, when the representatives of the Judenrat brought the collected gold to the regional commissar, they were told to come back the next day. The following day, the Judenrat received the commissar's answer: He said that according to his information, the Jews still had more gold, and the Judenrat had another two days to gather up the remaining gold that the Jews had hidden.

Once again, the representatives of the Judenrat gathered all the Jews and informed them of the regional commissar's answer. However, this time, they did not appeal to the Jews to hurry and turn over their gold and valuables as they had done before. Their faces reflected sorrow, and the people understood that nothing could stop the slaughter. Everyone stood around with their heads bowed, and before everyone dispersed, one of the Judenrat representatives said: "Maybe God will protect us from this great danger." This was May 6, 1942, two days before the great destruction in Lida.

Who Will Live and Who Will Die?

Early in the morning of May 8, 1942, armed SD units,[30] Lithuanian police, and White-Russian police surrounded the ghetto. Drunk and

30 The SD (Sicherheitsdienst) was the Nazi Party intelligence agency.

with savage rage, they tore into the ghetto, and with wild shouts of "Get out! Get out!" they attacked the bewildered Jews and drove them out of their houses. Anyone who hesitated to run out of the house—even for a second—was beaten with a rifle butt, thrown out onto the street, and driven toward the ghetto gate.

Both sides of the street were lined with Lithuanian policemen holding rifles in their hands, continually herding the Jews. At the gate, the Germans ordered us to line up in rows of four and to march in the direction of Kosharowa Street, with armed Lithuanian policemen lining the entire route. When the front row reached the point where the route forked into two roads, we stopped. The road to the right led to Kosharowa Street, and the road to the left led back to the ghetto. This was where the selection took place—who will live and who will die.[31]

Already waiting for us there were the executioners from the German police headquarters, led by the head of the SD together with the regional commissar Hanweg and his entire entourage. When the selections initially began, most of those with skilled-worker passes were sent to the left—to live—often along with their families. At the same time, many heartbreaking scenes played out, even for those who were fortunate enough to have a skilled-worker pass. If that person's family was deemed too large according to the murderers' judgment, the family would be torn apart. Part of the family would be sent to the left and the remainder to the right, to death. There were cases where the family refused to be separated, and they all went together to their death.

31 On May 8, 1942, the German Feldgendarmerie, policemen, and local auxiliaries surrounded the ghetto. All the Jews were ordered to assemble in the market square at 11:00 AM, but about 500 people managed to escape into the forest, and a further group of about 200 hid in the ghetto itself. The Lida *Gebietskommissar*, Hermann Hanweg, and his deputy for Jewish affairs, Leopold Windisch, then carried out a selection. Those who appeared fit for work were sent back to the ghetto, while the remaining Jews were held in the market square until evening without food or water. In the meantime, local peasants were forced to dig pits in the forest on the southeastern edge of the town. When the pits were ready, the Germans forced the Jews from the square to the pits and shot them all. According to estimates, 1,500 Jews with work permits remained in the ghetto while 5,700 Jews were killed in this murder operation.

I was among the last ones to reach the selection area, and I had no illusions that I—with my unskilled-worker pass—would be allowed to live. The lines moved slowly, bringing us closer to death with every step. However, as the back rows neared the selection area, the selection was abruptly stopped. The armed Lithuanians and Germans suddenly attacked us with their rifle butts and beat us mercilessly, driving us to the right into Kosharowa Street.

As we discovered later, the executioners had decided to keep alive only 1,300 of the over 7,000 Jews from the three Lida ghettos. Since the agreed-upon quota of Jews to remain alive had been filled, any further selection was no longer necessary. Thus, legitimate skilled workers, who had good passes and who would have certainly been sent to the left had they been in the front rows, were instead sent to the right, to their death. And so, some of those with "secure" passes went to the right alongside me.

We were herded to the area where those who had been sentenced to death were standing, and we joined that group. Shortly afterward, we were ordered to sit on the ground. All around us were the Lithuanian and White-Russian assistant murderers armed with machine guns. On the side stood two open trucks carrying barrels of lime, chlorine, and many shovels. The machine guns that were aimed at us did not rattle our nerves as much as the two trucks with the lime and the shovels.

All around us, stretching far and wide, were fields unto the horizon, where the borders of a forest could be clearly distinguished. I was sitting on the ground next to a man named Zakheim, the one-time director of the Vilna public bank on Pohulanka Street. I had known him in Vilna from before the war. He smoked one cigarette after another, which he himself had rolled, and he was beseeching God that the tobacco should last until his last breath. As we were talking, he took a gold watch out of his pocket and this is what he said to me: "You see this watch, Engelstern. My wife bought it for me as a wedding present. The murderers will not inherit this watch." And with these words, he smashed the gold watch against a rock and then buried it in the muddy ground. After that, Zakheim spoke his last words to me. He said, "I am no longer young, and I do not have the strength to escape. But you, Engelstern, are still young. You must not allow yourself to be led like an animal to the slaughter. Run away at the first opportunity and at least die an honorable death."

As soon as he concluded, we saw a middle-aged man pushing his way through the dense mass of people. He was a baker. We had considered him to be a dimwitted person in the ghetto. But this Jew, with his limited intelligence, understood better than others what had to be done in these last moments. He slowly shuffled through the mass of people, quietly urging us to act.

"Jews, you see now our situation in the world and what the Germans will soon do to us. We have only one way out. Let us pick up these rocks, throw them at the murderers, and run into the fields in all different directions. They will shoot at us. So what? Let them shoot. They are going to shoot us anyway. Let us at least die with honor and not like animals, and maybe some of us will be saved."

I was transported by his logical, intelligent words, but no one else was listening to him. Everyone was absorbed in their own thoughts. He did not stop pushing himself through the dense crowd of people, nor did he tire of repeating his words over and over. Fragments of conversations from the men and women sitting nearby reached my ears.

"Perhaps this is our fate because we sinned against God."

"Anyway, we won't be living much longer."

"We no longer have the strength to live and to see our children's suffering."

And other rationalizations such as, "Why should we save ourselves? Why cling to such a life? In just a short while, we will be delivered from this dark fate…"

The entire group of Jews—over 5,000 men, women, and children—sat there like condemned prisoners, resigned and with glazed eyes, waiting for the Hitlerists to free them from this hell on Earth. And when we heard the order to stand up and form rows of four, panic erupted. Mothers were searching for their children, and their shouts were loud enough to penetrate the heavens. Again, an order was heard: "March!"

It was at that very moment that a desire to live awakened inside me. All around were green fields and trees. Everything was blossoming, and just at that instant, we had to bid farewell to life.

We entered the narrow Kosharowa Street. Both sides of the street were densely lined with armed murderers. Our feet trudged through the deep mud of the unpaved road, every step forward bringing us closer to the last moment of our lives. When we had first lined up in rows of four, I made sure to be on the outside edge. My neighbors in the same row already knew of my plan, and they said that as soon as I ran from the row, they would immediately do the same. The Hitlerists were walking very close to me, and I was watching their every move. At the same time, I was scanning the area for a hole in the broken fence through which I could escape at the right moment. Soon, the long street with the houses would end, and my opportunity would be lost. My nerves were wound tight to the highest degree. Then, lightning fast, I decided: Now is the time! I ran out of the row and escaped through a hole in the fence. The other three in my row also began to run, and others from different rows ran too. The Germans opened a heavy volley of fire at us with their rifles and machine guns.

On the other side of the fence, I jumped down and lay in the wet mud. I held my breath, pushed my hat down to cover my face, spread out my arms flat on the ground, and remained completely motionless, as if I was dead. But this time, the bullets missed me. I lay there, sensing the murderers running nearby. When the shooting stopped and I could no longer hear the wild screams, I understood that the rows of condemned Jews had already passed through the street. I lifted my head slightly to see what was going on around me. I saw an outhouse nearby, and when I raised my head a little higher and saw that no one was around, I started to crawl on my stomach toward the outhouse and quickly sneaked in.

I peeked through the cracks in the outhouse walls, and all I saw were corpses across the whole field. My thoughts dulled entirely and, at first, I could not fully grasp the situation in which I had suddenly found myself. My clothes were drenched from lying in the wet mud, and I was shivering from the cold. The stench from the filled-up outhouse crept into my throat, making me feel like I was choking. Tears were flowing from my eyes and running down my muddy face, and I was wiping them with my muddy hands. How long this lasted, I don't remember. I only remember that the sound of heavy shooting brought me back to my senses. My tears soon stopped. I immediately realized that the last tragic act had begun. I started to imagine that in addition to hearing the gunfire, I was also hearing the cries of the dying victims.

The shooting did not cease, not even for a moment. At the same time, through the cracks in the outhouse, I caught sight of cars in which high-ranking Nazis apparently sat, driving to the killing site to observe how their comrades were exterminating the Jewish people. These cars went back and forth, bringing new people interested in observing Jewish blood flow.

In this way, minutes and hours passed and I continued to sit in that stench-filled outhouse, scared to go out for fear of being dragged to the pits. In the evening, the shooting stopped, a sign that the slaughter had ended. Indeed, I soon saw the cars returning from the killing site, and a little later came trucks filled with clothing. The victims had been forced to undress before the murderers killed them. I shuddered at this discovery. At the same time, I saw trucks driving to the houses where, just the night before, these Jews had been sleeping. The White-Russian police were carrying out all the belongings and driving away.

It was clear that I needed to disappear from the outhouse. If I didn't, I would end up in the murderers' clutches. As soon as it fell dark and the trucks had stopped coming to carry away the victims' belongings, I decided to leave my hideout. I surmised that they had surely posted guards in the streets to prevent the local peasants from looting the Jewish houses during the night. There was only one way left for me and that was through the fields. Hopefully, no one would notice me in the dark.

Good People

Crawling on my knees, I quickly slipped out of the outhouse. I crawled for a long time through the fields, which were still wet from the recently melted snow. I saw some low bushes ahead of me, and I decided to remain there until daylight. When it became a little lighter, I saw that I had covered a considerable distance overnight. I no longer had any yellow patches on me, having torn them off while in the outhouse. Moving quickly, I began to go deeper into the bushes. I picked out a thick bush and hid. I decided to stay there for as long as I could tolerate the hunger and thirst. Drained of all my strength, I collapsed and immediately fell asleep.

I was woken by loud barking, an indication that there were houses nearby. Thirst tormented me unbearably, but I did not dare to venture out of my hiding place. I decided to continue lying in this hideout until the next day. I lay there like that for three days. But I couldn't hold out any longer. It was now the third day that I had not drunk a drop of water.

The issue before me was where to go now. In my mind, at that moment, there was no question of going back to Lida. But before anything else, I needed to find a house where I could wash myself and somewhat clean my muddy clothes, so that I would not be suspected of being a runaway from the massacre. I left my hiding place and went to look for a house somewhere. I walked for around half a kilometer before seeing a house in the distance. I cautiously approached the house. A peasant woman was standing in front of the door. I approached her and asked if I could have a drink of water. She looked at me suspiciously but did not ask anything. She went into the house and soon returned with a ladle of water. I grabbed the water and greedily gulped it down. The peasant woman stood there stunned. It seemed that she had figured out from where I had come.

As I returned the ladle to her, I inquired if there were any visitors in her house and whether she would permit me to wash myself. Without any hesitation, she immediately invited me into the house. Once inside the house, I met her husband. Neither of them could stop looking at me, astonishment on both their faces. Suddenly, the peasant woman wrung her hands, crossed herself several times, and called out, "Oh, my God!" The peasant woman and her husband turned out to be very religious Catholics and very good people. I was extremely fortunate in happening upon such a house.

They told me to remove my muddied clothing and gave me a robe to put on. Then, they hung up my clothes over the heated oven to let them dry. The woman also heated up a large kettle of water so I could wash, and then she gave me food and drink. I thought to myself that, apparently, not all Christians are depraved human beings. After eating, I told them what had happened to me. When I finished, they told me to climb up to a spot above the oven and go to sleep.

I slept above the oven the entire night, and at daybreak, these good people told me to go into the barn and hide in the hay, just in case neighbors from the nearby houses might come in and see me. That could turn out to be very bad, both for them and for me. I immediately climbed down from above the oven and took my clothes, which had dried overnight, with me into the stable. Once I was in the stable, I cleaned the dirt off my clothes as best I could. As I was lying in the stable, I began to understand my dire situation. Who knows what would have happened to me had I not been so lucky as to happen upon such fine and honorable people? What do I do next? Where do I go?

When the Christian woman came to the stable and brought me something to eat, I unburdened myself, telling her what was bothering me. She said she was going into town soon and would inquire as to what was happening with the Jews. I breathed a little easier. In the evening, she returned with the news that the remaining Jews were in the ghetto located on Postawska Street. So, it seemed that my only way out was to go back to the ghetto where I had been before the slaughter.

However, getting back to the ghetto involved the danger of falling into the hands of the White-Russian police hooligans. Taking this danger into consideration, I decided that instead of going straight back to the ghetto, I would first go to the kitchen where I used to work, which was located outside the ghetto at that time. My thinking was that in the kitchen, I would be able to get more detailed information and then be able to enter the ghetto as part of the group of kitchen workers. The good Christian woman mapped out how I could get there using side roads. I thanked this genteel Christian lady wholeheartedly and set out on the side roads to return to the ghetto. I made it back there safely.

Testimony from the Murder Site

I found out what happened at the murder site from one of the nearly 6,000 people who had been condemned to death and who had witnessed the slaughter of the Lida Jews after I had fled. This was Motl (Mordechai) Gershowicz,[32] who had owned a bakery in Lida prior to the war. He had saved himself in an unbelievable way, and because of him we know the details of the horrific, brutal slaughter. What happened to him was somewhat similar to that of the Vilna paper merchant Shub, whose shop was on the corner of Zawalna and Stepono Streets. This was the shop where Hirsh Glick, the author of the song "Zog nit keynmol, az du geyst dem letstn veg,"[33] had worked. When Shub saw his own death approaching before his eyes during the liquidation of the ghetto, he offered a small bag of gold to one of the Gestapo murderers in exchange for his life. The Nazi took Shub with him to Gestapo headquarters, and after he received the gold, he led him down to the cellar and shot him.

Gershowicz described how the drunken murderers drove the condemned ones, under a hail of beatings, to the murder site, to two large open pits. A dense ring of armed Lithuanian and White-Russian police, under the supervision of an SD commandant, surrounded them. Forty people at a time were led to the pits. The murderers very carefully and precisely counted them, ordered them to undress, and told them to place their clothes in an indicated spot. Once they were naked, the SD commandant activated the machine guns. In this way, the German beasts systematically herded one group after another to the pits, and a volley of bullets completed the task. Gershowicz told us about the heartrending scenes that played out before the unfortunate victims took their last breath. He spoke of the helpless screams of the mothers when the murderers tore their little children from their arms and flung them into the pits.

He then told us of a Vilna Jew called Minikes, who was also at the murder site with his family and whom I actually knew from both

32 The baker Motl Gershowicz was born in Lida in 1904.

33 Hirsh Glick was a Yiddish poet born in Vilna in 1922. His most famous work is the song "Zog nit keynmol, az du geyst dem lestn veg" (Never Say You Are on the Final Road), also known as "The Partisans' Song," which he wrote in 1943 while he was in the Vilna ghetto. The song became the anthem of the Jewish partisan movement. In the summer of 1944, after escaping from the Goldpiltz concentration camp in Estonia to the nearby forests, Glick was caught and executed by the Germans.

the Vilna and the Lida ghettos. Seeing that the last minute of his life was approaching, he called out in desperation to a German standing near him and told him that he had buried some gold in the ghetto and would give him the gold if the German would let him live. The German removed him and his wife from the line and told them to stand on the side.

Gershowicz overheard what the Vilna Jew had said to the Nazi and repeated the same story to a different German, who removed Gershowicz from the line and stood him next to the Minikes family. After a short while, the two armed Germans accompanied them to the ghetto to retrieve the buried gold. Minikes lived in the ghetto on Kosharowa Street, and since this was not far from the murder site, they went to his place first. Gershowicz, on the other hand, said that his gold was in a different section of the ghetto, so the second German went there with him.

After walking a short distance, Gershowicz heard several gunshots coming from the direction of Minikes and the German. The situation became quite clear to him, and Gershowicz immediately thought of a plan. He began to lead the German from one place to another, saying that he couldn't remember exactly where he had buried the gold. His idea was to delay and gain some time, but the German finally got fed up with trailing after the Jew and ordered him to march ahead. Gershowicz, sensing the German's intent, began to run away as fast as he could. The German opened fire on him, and Gershowicz was hit and fell to the ground. He was lying in a pool of blood.

Just as his escape from the pits was dramatic, so too were the events that followed. He was clandestinely brought back into the ghetto, where he lingered between life and death for many months. The famous Lida surgeon, Dr. Chaim Miasnik, performed a complicated operation on him and secretly tended to him until he and his family escaped from the ghetto to join the partisans in the Lipichanskaya Pushcha.[34] A short time later, Gershowicz recovered and also fled to the forest.

34 Pushcha means a large, dense forest area.

There were many like Minikes and Gershowicz who, right up to the last moment, did not lose the will to save themselves. However, even the cleverest ideas would sometimes go awry, and only fate determined the outcome. The fact that I managed to come out alive during that black period is just another example of that truth. Who can understand the ways of Divine Providence?

Back in the Lida Ghetto

The workers in the kitchen immediately noticed that I had come from "there," and even before they had a chance to ask me anything, the women quickly found a yellow rag and cut out yellow patches, pinning them to me on both the front and the back before the non-Jewish manager of the kitchen came down. The woodcutters took me in, and I helped to chop and saw wood. From that moment on, my subsequent ghetto life was sealed.

As I sawed the wood, I told them about everything that had happened to me during the previous few days. They calmed me down and assured me that I would be able to stay in the ghetto legally, just like the others. When the manager came down, the workers told her that I had been sent by the Judenrat to help saw wood. The fact is, she needed more people, but the Judenrat did not have enough workers to send. She was, therefore, pleased with my arrival as she would have another free laborer.

With great impatience, I counted the hours until the day would end so that I could return to the ghetto and find out who was still alive from the house where I had lived. When I entered the house that evening, none of the people who I had previously known were there. Of the twenty-three people who had lived in the three rooms of the house, I was the only survivor. I immediately felt like a stranger among these unfamiliar people, people who, before the slaughter, had lived in a different ghetto. I also found very little of my belongings and clothing.

I returned to the Lida ghetto four days after the selection and the subsequent reestablishment of the "new" ghetto. Only 1,300 Jews remained alive in the ghetto following the selection. Several days later, twenty more people returned, people who had somehow saved themselves by various means. Just twenty! This was all that was left of the nearly 6,000 Jews who the murderers had herded to the pits.

Life in the ghetto went on as "normal," as if nothing had happened just four days earlier. The sorrow and pain from the loss of families and loved ones were carried deep within the hearts of the survivors. However, Hanweg's orders once again had to be carried out promptly, and so there was no time to mourn those who had perished. There was already a new Judenrat and a new police commandant in charge of the newly established ghetto police, and as before, Jews went to work outside the ghetto every morning.

Across the street from my house in the ghetto, there lived a Lida family—the Tzigelnitskis—who had the entire house to themselves. The family consisted of the father, the mother, three grown daughters, and a daughter-in-law with her three-year-old daughter. In the ghetto, the father was known as "Henech the Yellow," and he was a lathe operator by trade. This family knew me from before, and I had often visited them in the evening after work. The family was saved from the massacre thanks to two of the daughters who worked at the police headquarters doing laundry. Later, however, when the Lida ghetto was liquidated in September 1943, they were all taken away to be murdered. Only one daughter managed to save herself by escaping from the train. Later, she joined the Bielski partisan group, and after the war, she made *aliya* to Israel.

When they saw me back in the ghetto after the massacre, the Tzigelnitskis were overjoyed that I had survived, and they reacted as if I was a member of their family. Seeing that I was forlorn, living among strangers in my house, they invited me to stay with them in their home, and they actually adopted me as part of their family. I remained with them until the day I left for the forest.

After working in the kitchen that first day, I decided that this would be a good place to work. So, I asked the Judenrat to assign me there, and they agreed. The next morning, I went to work in the kitchen, which turned out to be my last job assignment in the ghetto. As I have previously mentioned, the kitchen manager was a middle-aged Polish woman. Her family name was Tomasevich. She was a religious Catholic but an antisemite. Her husband was a member of the reactionary Polish Endecja party.[35] When the Soviets occupied Lida in 1939, her husband, among others, was taken to Siberia. She believed that the Jews were responsible for her husband's deportation to Siberia, and from then on, she had a burning hatred of Jews.

This antisemitic woman was the sole boss in charge of the food portions assigned to the Jews that she received from the town administration for the ghetto kitchen. The portions of grain and potatoes that the Nazis allocated to each person in the ghetto were much smaller than the portions given to Christians. To make matters worse, the heartless manager stole half of this lesser amount and sold it, earning a good deal of money at the expense of the hungry Jews. A fiery rage burned within me toward this evil, supposedly religious Catholic woman who was stealing from the defenseless Jews and letting them go hungry. But what could we do about it? Our lives were in her hands, something she was well aware of, and she excelled at using her power for her own personal gain.

One day, the cook fell sick and could no longer come to work, so a new cook was needed. When I arrived at work that morning, the boss came over to me and said, "Lazar, you will be the cook." I replied by saying I didn't know how to do this job, but she stamped her foot and shouted angrily, "Quiet, you bloody dog!" She then told the women who were peeling potatoes to show me what to do. The women, seeing my frightened face and helplessness, calmed me down. They promised to help me and assured me that I would learn the work just like the previous cook had done. He also did not know what to do at first. So, from then on, I was the cook. It took a couple of days, but I soon learned the job. Few people in the ghetto had known me before, but soon, everyone in the ghetto recognized me and already knew my name—Lazar the Cook. Everyone suddenly started calling me by that name.

35 The National Democratic Party, known as Endecja, was the most important Polish nationalist party. Founded in 1893 by Roman Dmowski (1864–1939), it placed the fight against Jews at the center of its program.

In the same week that the Germans carried out their gruesome slaughter of the Lida Jews, they did the same in every town that fell under the control of the regional commissar Hanweg. Selections also took place in those places. In the ten towns that comprised the Lida region, which was estimated to have about 30,000 Jews at that time, the murderers selected approximately 2,000 of the most important tradesmen, such as tailors, shoemakers, and mechanics, to keep alive. Simultaneously, an order was issued to make these towns *Judenrein* (cleansed of Jews) and to deport the remaining Jews to the Lida ghetto.

Now, there was one remaining ghetto in the entire region, and it contained over 3,000 Jews from both the Lida ghetto and Jews from the surrounding towns. The wounds of these newly arrived Jews were still fresh, and they agonized over their recently lost families. No one could console them, but they were not alone in their grief. The wounds of the Lida Jews had also not healed following the slaughter.

The crowded conditions in the ghetto were now much worse than they had been before the mass murder. The same number of houses that had previously housed the already large number of ghetto inhabitants now had to accommodate the new arrivals as well. We pressed ourselves together a little closer to make room for everyone. In addition, the workshops, which had lost so many workers during the slaughter, were now starting to fill with new workers. Slowly, we adjusted to the new situation, and life in the ghetto became "normal."

The change was also immediately felt in the kitchen where I worked because there were more people to feed. I now had to cook two large pots twice a day—at noon and in the evening. When the workers left work, they would take their portions of soup with them to the ghetto. I labored well beyond my strength, but I was content. However, one thing distressed me greatly. The antisemitic manager was stealing from us, and because of this, I had to dole out watery soup to hungry people. I was helpless against her, until all of a sudden, a change for the better took place.

Among the newly arrived Jews, there were a small number of *yeshiva*[36] boys. They were refugees from Radun[37] and survivors of the slaughter that had occurred there. One of these *yeshiva* boys came to work in the kitchen. This *yeshiva* boy, whose name was Chaim, accomplished wonders and brought about a complete reversal in the behavior of the heartless Polish kitchen manager.

I will not describe Chaim's *frumkeit*[38] and will only say that the kitchen workers considered him to be a holy person. We were uplifted by his faith. He would always comfort me, saying, "I tell you, Lazar, we will live to see the salvation very soon." The antisemitic manager also noticed his piety right away, and from the very first day, her attitude toward him was completely different than toward the rest of us.

Chaim found out about the vile acts of the corrupt kitchen manager, and he would physically tremble whenever we spoke of her thievery. One time, she approached him with a request to beseech God on behalf of her husband in captivity. At the very least, she wanted to hear some news that he was alive. Chaim did not respond to this, however it just so happened that shortly after she made her request to Chaim, she received a telegram from her husband, saying that he was alive and well in Turkey.

The woman almost went crazy with joy. I don't know whether she believed Chaim had "prayed to God for her husband," but the result of this telegram was very good for all the hungry Jews in the ghetto. Something had happened to affect her conscience, and from then on, she entrusted Chaim with the key to the storage facility where the produce was kept, as well as the key to the cellar where the potatoes were stored. Chaim now made sure that enough grain and potatoes were in the pots, and I was able to cook a thick soup with which the Jews

36 A *yeshiva* is the traditional Jewish educational institution focused on the study of rabbinic literature, primarily the Talmud and Halacha, while Torah and Jewish philosophy are studied in parallel.

37 The *yeshiva* referred to here is probably the Radun (or Radin) Yeshiva, also known as Yeshiva Chafetz Chaim of Radun. For more on Radun, see the foreword "Between Survival and Resistance" of this volume.

38 *Frumkeit* refers to a person's level of observance of Jewish religious law.

in the ghetto could still their hunger. I was then able to feel some sort of satisfaction from my hard work. It was no longer difficult for me to stand in front of the large boiling pot, enveloped in steam, stirring the soup with the large wooden ladle to prevent it from sticking to the bottom and burning.

At the same time, Chaim also persuaded the kitchen manager Tomasevich to allow him to cook a separate small pot of soup for his *yeshiva* friends so that they would not have to eat from a non-kosher pot. Actually, the soup was cooked without any fat at all, just some meager grains and potatoes. However, on the rare occasion when a "holiday" occurred, she would receive bones to put in the pot, and the *yeshiva* boys would not eat the soup on such occasions. On Friday, for example, he would also cook for the *yeshiva* boys for *Shabbos*,[39] and before sunset, he would carry a pail full of soup back to the ghetto. There was no one like him. He had certainly earned greater merit than I to be granted life by God.

39 *Shabbos* (Shabbat, Saturday) is the Jewish Sabbath.

CHAPTER THREE

ESCAPE TO THE FOREST

Where Do We Get Weapons?

One morning, we awoke to go to work, and we discovered that during the night, the previously mentioned Dr. Miasnik and his family had disappeared from the ghetto. This doctor, a surgeon, was famous not only in Lida but also throughout the entire surrounding area. Even the Germans considered him to be the best doctor in the Lida military hospital where he worked, and it seemed certain that he would remain alive. Dr. Miasnik's disappearance from the ghetto caused quite a stir. From this incident, the ghetto inhabitants inferred that it was undeniably the right time to escape to the forest.

There soon began much frenzied activity to obtain weapons. Within the ghetto, there were already Jews who had become dealers and, of course, they earned a sizable income in this way. It also opened up a new stream of income for the Poles. They already had the sources from which to obtain weapons, and the ghetto dealers were able to provide a weapon to anyone who had the money to pay the outrageous prices. For example, a rifle—called a "long one" in ghetto lingo—cost between 30,000 and 35,000 rubles. A revolver—a "short one"—cost between 15,000 and 20,000 rubles. As I said, outrageous prices that only a few Jews could afford.

There were, however, other ways of arming oneself with a rifle or a revolver. I knew of two mechanics who secretly obtained a rifle made from parts they had collected and then assembled in the ghetto workshops. Even inside the German police headquarters itself, a Lida Jew called Leibke Orzechovski, a mechanic whose job was to repair the weapons in those workshops, assembled a rifle from parts that were just lying around. With this rifle, he later went into the forest together with his brother and mother.

Another distinct problem was smuggling a weapon into the ghetto, and an even more difficult issue was finding a hiding place for it until the escape into the forest. Hiding a "long one" or a "short one" endangered the lives of everyone who lived in the house. Therefore, one can only imagine the responsibility involved in hiding any kind of weapon, and it was also not easy to find a suitable hiding place.

There were also those who had not managed to obtain a weapon in order to escape to the forest, so they skulked around looking for a hidden "long one" or "short one." And when they discovered a hidden weapon, they simply swiped it and disappeared with it. When the owner of the weapon realized that he had been wronged, there was nothing he could do about it and had to keep quiet. Such an incident actually happened in the courtyard where Henech the Yellow lived. There was a "long one" hidden in the cellar of the courtyard, and someone stole it and disappeared from the ghetto.

Regardless of these issues, undercover operations continued in the ghetto as people tried to obtain a weapon. The prices for the "long ones" and the "short ones" fluctuated, depending on the demand. If on a given day demand increased, the price would rise, and if on another day the demand went down, the price would drop.

Gradually and covertly, people began to disappear from the ghetto. The winter of 1942 began very early with extremely low temperatures, and this was, in fact, one of the main reasons most people put off their escape to the forest, even those who already had weapons. At that time, no one had any idea of how it would be possible to survive winter in the forest. No one had received any news from the few people who had already gone to the forest. The ghetto itself was also ostensibly calm at this time, and the optimists added to this calm by convincing themselves and others that the ghetto was "secure," more so than it had been previously because "the Germans needed Jewish workers, and the Jewish skilled workers provided great assistance to the army on the battlefields."

Henech the Yellow, with whom I lived, belonged to this group of optimists. He worked as a lathe operator in the workshops of the ghetto and therefore had a "good" pass. "See," he used to say with joy, "today again, more wagons arrived with work for the shoemakers, the tailors, and the other guilds, more work than it's possible to complete even in a year. So, isn't this a sign that the ghetto is secure?" He would be cheerful and speak with great fervor about how the regional commissar had visited the workshops, assuring everyone that there was nothing to be afraid of and that they just had to work diligently and everything would be all right—there would not be a repeat of what had happened previously in the Lida ghetto.

When I recall the discussions about whether to go into the forest or not, which truly grated on me at the time, I painfully relive this delusion, because such opportunities to escape into the forest did not exist in Vilna, Białystok, and other ghettos. And regarding Henech the Yellow, what can one say? He and his family had the absolute best opportunity to flee. He had plenty of money to procure weapons for himself, and he also had connections. All those who subsequently led people out of the ghetto and into the forest had been visitors at his house.

Hundreds of people like Henech let this chance—which did not last very long—slip by because of their optimism. There were some excellent opportunities to escape from the Lida ghetto and enter the forest, but people did not take advantage of them at the appropriate time and in its fullest measure. From spring 1943, for example, the mood in the ghetto totally changed and became more pessimistic, causing a large number of Jews to vanish from the ghetto. But when summer arrived, the stream into the forest halted for the time being due to a variety of reasons. Furthermore, the unexpected liquidation of the Lida ghetto in September 1943 wiped out the many hundreds of Jews who were already armed with weapons and who were ready to enter the forest.[40] It is extremely difficult to speak of this now.

However, in the meantime, a group of people would gather in Henech the Yellow's house every evening. Among those who visited often were two brothers: Ignatz and Avraham Feldan, refugees who were stuck in Lida after a successful escape from their hometown of Łódź. Only a few people in the ghetto knew that the older brother Ignatz had already been with the partisans in the forest for several months and, of course, Henech's family knew of this too. Every day, the younger brother Avraham would wait for Ignatz to come and take him out of the ghetto. Also waiting was Ignatz's beloved girlfriend Mashke Szewachowicz,[41] the daughter of a well-known Lida family who later joined the Bielski partisans. Later, I will return to this family and to the two brothers, Ignatz and Avraham Feldan.

The First Greeting from the Forest

It was an extremely cold night in the beginning of February 1943. Suddenly, in the middle of the night, we heard a light tapping on the window. We were all jolted awake from our sleep, and we ran over to the window, thinking that there was probably going to be some kind of trouble again. The windowpanes were covered with ice, and we could not see anything. "Open the door quickly," we heard someone call out in Yiddish.

40 The final liquidation of the Lida ghetto occurred on September 18, 1943. On that day, the ghetto was surrounded by police, and the Jews were driven to the railway station, loaded onto railroad cars, and sent on two separate trains to the concentration and death camp of Majdanek and to the death camp of Sobibór, where virtually all of them were annihilated.

41 Mashke Szewachowicz was born in Lida in 1924. She escaped from the ghetto to the forests with her family and joined the Iskra *otriad*, where she was a nurse.

When I went to open the door, Ignatz was there! I let him in and immediately bolted the door behind him. He came into the house, and we saw his attire and the revolver visible at his side. We were frightened, but Ignatz understood our anxiety and immediately said that we did not have to be afraid because he had come through the barbed-wire fences at the back. He said that no one had seen him and nobody else had to know he was here. These words calmed us down, but no one went back to sleep. We were all in our underwear, and we sat down on our beds to listen to Ignatz tell us about partisan life in the forest.

We listened to Ignatz in amazement. His words surprised us—it was so different from what we had previously imagined about living in the forest during the winter. I recall that in my eyes, Ignatz seemed like a hero. Oh, how I envied him at that moment. We were all so caught up in his narrative that we didn't even notice that the day was dawning. Everyone began hurrying to get ready for work, while Ignatz crept up into the attic, took a warm blanket with him, and went to sleep. On their way to work, Henech's daughters notified Avraham and Mashke of Ignatz's arrival.

The following night, all three were ready to leave. Mashke and Avraham, of course, already had "short ones"—revolvers. We said goodbye to them, and just as nobody had seen or heard Ignatz arrive, so it was that no one saw the three of them disappear. That is what we in Henech's house believed. However, the next morning, after their departure, just about everyone in the ghetto already knew everything, and it became an open secret.

Ignatz was part of a Russian partisan group that belonged to the Iskra *otriad*, and he took Avraham and Mashke there. However, Mashke was not destined to use her revolver for very long to avenge the spilling of Jewish blood. Her fate was to die by a bullet from a Russian partisan who was a member of the Iskra *otriad*. According to conjecture, this Russian partisan was interested in Mashke, but she ignored him. She was sent on a mission with a group of partisans from which she never returned. A traitor's bullet pierced her heart, and so it was destined for Ignatz to lose his beloved girl in the forest.[42] Mashke was not the only

42 It appears that Mashke was killed on August 26, 1943, by the Lithuanian police

Jewish girl who died at the hands of an antisemitic partisan. I remember many such cases where Jewish partisans had to fight both the Nazis and the Russian partisan hooligans, partisans with whom they were fighting shoulder-to-shoulder against a mutual enemy.

Right after Ignatz and his brother Avraham left, a restless feeling came over me. That first greeting from the forest made such an impression on me that I couldn't sleep at night and could only think about the forest. I was totally obsessed with the idea of going into the forest and could not focus on my work in the kitchen. The other workers noticed my restlessness and started asking questions as to whether I had heard bad news in the ghetto. But all this thinking made me realize that there was no possibility for me to join the partisans. I didn't have any money to get some kind of weapon and, according to Ignatz, without my own weapon, the partisans would not accept me. And so, I went around full of empty dreams.

At that time in the Lida ghetto, almost nothing was known about the Bielski brothers and their partisan group.[43] It is possible that some

following a denunciation. See Yehiel Gernstein and Moshe Kahanovitz, eds., *Lexicon Hagvura: Partizanim Velohamei Mahteret Yehudim Be'azurim Hama'aravim shel Brit Hamo'atzot*, vol. 2 (Hebrew) (Jerusalem: Yad Vashem, 1965), p. 188.

43 The Bielski partisans were a group of Jewish partisans who operated in the forests of Belorussia during World War II. The group provided a haven for Jews fleeing Nazi persecution and were known for their efforts to both rescue Jews and launch guerrilla attacks on German forces and their collaborators. The group was led by the Bielski brothers—Tuvia, Asael, Alexander (Zus, Zusye), and their younger brother Aron (Arczyk)—four out of the twelve children in their family. Tuvia Bielski (b. 1906) was the commander of the partisan unit. In the summer of 1941, after the German invasion of the Soviet Union, he joined his family in his hometown of Stankiewicze, near Nowogródek in Western Belorussia. Following the murder of his parents and other relatives, he escaped with three of his brothers to the nearby forests where he commanded the Bielski family camp. After the war, Tuvia Bielski immigrated to *Eretz Israel*, and in 1956, he immigrated to the United States where he settled in New York. He passed away in 1987, and a year later, his remains were brought to Israel to be buried in Jerusalem. Asael Bielski (b. 1908) was Tuvia's deputy in the forest and was responsible for the day-to-day life of the unit and its fighters. After liberation from the forest, he was drafted into the Red Army and was killed on February 7, 1945. After his death, his wife Chaya, who was pregnant

people did, in fact, know something, but they kept it to themselves and were afraid to speak of it. Later, information about a Jewish commander and his Jewish partisans began to spread. However, it was considered a vague rumor mixed in with pure fantasy.

As it turned out, all this undercover talk in people's homes did, in fact, have some basis of truth. Tuvia Bielski had sent agents to Lida and Nowogródek to take Jews out of the ghetto and bring them to the forest. All this had to be done with utmost secrecy. But how long could something like this be kept secret in the ghetto, when even a wink in someone's home could be an indication that something unusual was going on? It did not take long before the secret was out.

As soon as it became known in the Lida ghetto that there was a Jewish partisan *otriad* led by a Jewish commander, most of those who had fled to the forest began to gravitate toward the Bielski brothers. It also didn't take long before people returned from the Bielski *otriad* to the ghetto to bring the rest of their family members and their friends or neighbors to the forest. From then on, both large and small groups began to leave the ghetto. Naturally, all of this went on "in secret," but the entire ghetto knew about it.

People began to disappear from the ghetto, and there was much talk and agitation in peoples' homes, which brought with it a justified foreboding. This would not be kept secret from the German authorities for long because everyone who had disappeared had been working in German units, and those Germans would certainly inform the authorities that their Jewish workers had not come to work. This was perfectly clear to everyone in the ghetto, and they were very afraid of the consequences.

when her husband was drafted into the Red Army, immigrated to *Eretz Israel* where their daughter Asaela was born. Alexander (Zus) (b. 1912) was the intelligence officer of the unit and participated in many combat operations. After the war, in October 1945, he immigrated to *Eretz Israel* and settled in Holon, but later immigrated to the United States. He passed away in 1986 in Brooklyn, leaving behind three sons. Aron (Arczyk) (b. 1927) was the youngest of the Bielski family. He witnessed the murder of his relatives, lost his ability to speak, and remained mute for two years. Nevertheless, he became a fighter in his brothers' partisan unit. After the war, he immigrated to *Eretz Israel* but later moved to the United States to be with his brothers.

At that time, I recall the strong disagreements between the pessimists—those who were preparing to leave for the forest—and the so-called optimists. The optimists shouted, waving their hands: "You will see. You will bring disaster down on the ghetto if you leave for the forest while we remain here. Don't you care at all what will happen to us?" However, the other side had an answer for them: "Who is stopping you from going to the forest? Do what we are doing. We don't want these murderers to drive us to the slaughter like animals for a second time."

This exchange of words was what I heard every evening in Henech the Yellow's house. Many of the optimists certainly understood that their claim was not legitimate. They were making this argument simply because they could not bring themselves to leave the ghetto. For some, it was not possible for the entire family to leave together, and they did not want to part from their families, along with various other reasons.

Behind a Threefold Barbed-Wire Fence

One day, the regional commissar sent for the chairman of the Judenrat and demanded that he give a short and precise response to the following questions: Why are Jews vanishing from the ghetto, and where are they going? The Judenrat had prepared a perfect excuse for this and responded that all those who had disappeared are apparently Vilnaites, and they thought that they would be better off in the Vilna ghetto, so they probably went there. It is difficult to say whether the regional commissar believed this excuse. It is more likely that he had already figured out to where the Jews were disappearing, and this resulted in consequences for the ghetto that soon occurred.

A few days later, the Judenrat received an order from the police headquarters that within twenty-four hours, they had to report the names of those who had disappeared from the ghetto. One can only imagine the kind of turmoil this order generated and the kind of fear that enveloped the ghetto. This order actually caused even more people to flee into the forest and, of course, the Judenrat had to report those who had vanished. It was not even possible to hide this for more than twenty-four hours because the work units had also been ordered to immediately report any Jews who had not shown up for work.

When Hanweg saw that the number of people disappearing from the ghetto was growing, he instituted additional methods to stop this flight from the ghetto. He issued an order to the Judenrat to build a high, threefold barbed-wire fence surrounding the ghetto. The order stated that the work must be completed quickly, and barbed wire and wooden poles were supplied shortly after. The Judenrat selected a special brigade of Jews to work on this fence. On Sundays, even more people were added to the group since they were free from their regular work. Those who were building this fence had the feeling that they were digging their own graves. The ground was frozen, and it was very difficult to dig holes for the fence posts. But despite these difficulties, the number of poles installed increased every day, and the threefold fence enclosed the ghetto ever more tightly.

However, Hanweg had thought up another way to prevent more disappearances. Until that time, there had not been any White-Russian police stationed in the ghetto or at the gate—only ghetto police. The White-Russian police only showed up when the workers returned from work to catch anyone who was attempting to smuggle food into the ghetto. But as soon as the threefold fence was completed, the regional commissar sent in a guard unit consisting of members of the White-Russian fascist youth organization, in which the most depraved young thugs of the Polish and White-Russian population had enlisted. They wore uniforms of coarse white linen and hats shaped like a goose's beak, and so they became known as "white geese."

These hooligans, blood-enemies of the Jews, became our ghetto bosses. Day and night, they stood watch at the gate and, armed with guns and rifles, patrolled the ghetto. In this way, a new torment was added to our fear and suffering that we had to put up with every day. We also understood that now we could no longer smuggle any food into the ghetto nor take clothing out of the ghetto to sell. And as for obtaining weapons, that was obviously out of the question. Furthermore, we feared that in the future, people would no longer be able to sneak through the barbed wire at night and escape into the forest. After all, escaping through three fences is far more difficult than escaping through just one.

From then on, we did not have another peaceful moment in the ghetto. The "white" hooligans zealously instilled fear in the Jews in every possible way. For no reason at all, they kept up continuous gunfire throughout the night. There were quite a few instances when, out of necessity, someone left his house and was shot on his doorstep, despite the fact that it was before the ten o'clock curfew. According to the guards, however, it was past the curfew. That is why we were afraid to leave the house as soon as evening arrived. Yet, we also adjusted to this new situation, and we managed to cope with the "white geese." The escape activity did not cease, and people continued to leave the ghetto to head for the forest.

The Jewish ghetto police in Lida were not as despised by the Lida Jews as much as the Jewish police in Vilna were despised by the Vilna Jews, for example.[44] Nevertheless, I have nothing good to say about even the best ghetto policeman just for this reason alone: the Germans did not force anyone to become a policeman. The best policeman in the ghetto was, after all, still serving the Nazis and carrying out their orders against his own brothers and sisters. I have no interest in depicting the Lida ghetto police in a better light. I simply want to describe factually how the process of escaping from the ghetto to the forest took place as a result of this newly created situation.

The last commandant of the Lida ghetto police was Lazar Stolitski, whose brother had been a teacher at the Vilna Real Gymnasium. He had translated *Krylov's Fables*[45] into Yiddish, which I believe was published by my brother-in-law Shloyme Bastomski's publishing house. Stolitski was an intelligent and unassuming person, and I often wondered how such a person had convinced himself to take such a position in the ghetto police. He was also one of the visitors at Henech the Yellow's house from time to time.

44 The commander of the Vilna ghetto police Salk (Salek) Dessler was a hated man among the ghetto Jews, who considered him to be a Nazi collaborator.

45 He refers here to the well-known fables of the Russian author Ivan Krylov (1769–1844).

This Lazar Stolitski soon figured out a scheme by which people wishing to escape to the forest could leave the ghetto. When a group was planning to leave the ghetto on a given night, the group leader would notify Lazar Stolitski in advance. Bottles of liquor were stored in the Judenrat office, and Stolitski would invite the "white geese" in for a drink. These hooligans could never say no to a drink. Of course, Lazar Stolitski was not in the least bit stingy in pouring the drinks. While they were in the office guzzling liquor, one of the ghetto policemen would signal to the waiting group, and in the blink of an eye, they would escape through the rear barbed-wire fence, which had been previously "fixed" so that they could crawl out without leaving any sign of an escape. Lazar Stolitski had also intended to leave later for the forest but waited too long, and when the liquidation of the ghetto suddenly happened, he went to his death along with all the others.

In the meantime, about half a kilometer from the ghetto, there was a farm called Pyaruv (Pyar). The Russians had nationalized this particular farm, and when the Nazis came, Hanweg considered this farm to be his own property. In the ghetto, it was known as "the regional commissar's estate." Jews from the ghetto also worked there doing various tasks. The partisans had cast an eye on this estate, and one night they paid it a visit. They picked out the best horses and wagons, filled up the wagons with whatever was worth taking, and took it all away.

When the Jews from the ghetto arrived at work the next morning, the custodian was shaking, as if he had chills and a fever, due to the fearful experience he had just lived through. One can only imagine how ticked off Hanweg and his gang were by this daring piece of work that the partisans had carried out against "his estate," right under his nose. Well, in the ghetto we rubbed our hands with glee! However, after this incident, Hanweg sent a group of armed White-Russian policemen to stand guard there.

Proud and Fearless

It was the beginning of March 1943. The sun was melting away the snow, and it smelled like spring. But in our hearts and souls, it felt like autumn. Sadness lay across my face. I lived with just one thought: How can I find a way to get myself out of the ghetto and to join the partisans in the forest?

Suddenly, in a totally unexpected fashion, salvation arrived. At that time, people from the forest had started to come to the ghetto more often to take their family members out. Contact between the forest and the ghetto increased with each passing day. There were also messengers sent to the ghetto by the partisan commander Tuvia Bielski. They started to come more often than before to take out Jews, regardless of age or whether they had a weapon. Of course, all this was shrouded in secrecy. Since the White-Russian hooligans were constantly in the ghetto day and night, a way had to be found for the agents from the forest to maintain contact with the ghetto without being noticed by the sentries.

There was a certain spot in Lida with a large garden and hothouses in which various types of vegetables grew. Hanweg had appropriated this garden for his own use. Several men and women from the ghetto worked in this garden, cultivating various sorts of vegetables that were provided daily to the regional commissar and his group. The supervisor of this garden and its workers was a Lida Jew named Mawnes. He had a small house there, and he had received permission from the regional commissar to live there because he was responsible for everything that went on in the garden. Later, the partisans from the forest would hide in this garden, since they could not get into the ghetto during the day because of the careful watch of the "white geese." This was also the place where Mawnes's acquaintances and friends had hidden weapons. Mawnes and his wife later joined Bielski's *otriad* and remained there until the liberation.

One day, Avraham Feldan came from the forest to extract his family members from the ghetto. When I returned from work that evening, I met Avraham in our house, the home of Henech the Yellow. I was soon imploring him to take me to the forest as well. At first, he was reluctant because I did not have a weapon, but since he knew me well from the time he had been a daily visitor to Henech's house, he finally agreed and told me to get ready to leave the following night. I immediately began to sew a rucksack from a linen sack that Henech's wife had given me. The house was full of visiting *kibitzers*, but now I was no longer interested in listening to their conversations. I was busy sewing the rucksack, and my thoughts were now in a different realm.

I went to work in the morning as usual, but I could not work. I was dropping everything that I touched. The women who were peeling potatoes noticed immediately that something was wrong. I told them that I was not feeling well, however I confided my secret to Chaim, the *yeshiva* boy. He encouraged me, telling me that I should just have faith in God and all would be fine. I was counting the minutes, waiting for the day to finally end. When I entered our house later that day, Avraham informed me that he already had a group of over twenty people and that we would be leaving around midnight—as soon as Lazar Stolitski gave the signal. I was to be ready some time before that. I had already prepared the absolute minimum of clothing and a few other necessities.

That evening, Avraham Feldan was at our house, and the others in the group waited in nearby houses. Shortly after midnight, a ghetto policeman—the messenger from Lazar Stolitski—came with the "signal" for us to leave immediately. Literally within seconds, we were all in a corner of the ghetto at the barbed-wire fences. That same night, another group was also leaving. The leader of this second group, which consisted of more than thirty people, was the previously mentioned young man from Lida named Leibke Orzechovski. In the ghetto, he was known by the nickname "Leibke the Katzap," and he was a strong, heavyset fellow. The group that he was leading was already the second one he was taking out of the ghetto. And so, all together, including Avraham's group, we were a total of almost sixty people—the largest group until that point to leave the ghetto in one night.

I remember that the moon shone brightly that night, and we were therefore fearful in those first few minutes. To this very day, I remember the magnificent scene ahead of me when I ran to the barbed-wire fence. There stood a group of people, some with rifles and revolvers, the very same people who only moments earlier had been wearing yellow patches and were now standing proud and fearless, with weapons in their hands and ready to fight. I felt a strong respect for these audacious youths and, at the same time, envied their good fortune that they had weapons.

On one side of the barbed-wire fence were the "white geese" in the ghetto, and on the other side was the regional commissar's Pyaruv farm, just a few hundred meters from the ghetto, where the White-Russian police stood watch. And here, between them, stood our armed group. I barely had time to take in this most unusual scene before Avraham and Leibke the Katzap drew their revolvers from their pockets and took command, informing us that from now on, we must follow their instructions. Then, they pointed to a hole in the barbed-wire fence and told us to crawl through it. They both stood there, revolvers in hand, until everyone had crawled through before arranging the fence to hide the hole. On the other side, there was a small stream that we crossed before we found ourselves in the fields of the farm. It was here that we heard the loud barking of dogs. Avraham and Leibke the Katzap issued an order: "Start moving, guys!"

Well, well, we started to move quickly across the wet fields, which were very muddy from the newly melted snow. We mustered as much strength as we could to distance ourselves from the ghetto as fast as possible. Had it not been for the abovementioned partisan ambush at the farm, the dogs' barking would surely have drawn the Germans' attention. After the ambush, however, the police who were guarding the farm at the time were afraid for their own skin and chose to ignore the barking.

For approximately three or four hours, we traipsed through fields and trails until we came upon a dirt road. We had barely walked half a kilometer on this open road when we encountered two partisans on horseback. This was a *razvedka*[46] from a Russian *otriad*. They stopped us and asked who we were. Our commanders explained everything to them. The partisans wished us luck, and we continued on our way. It was not unusual for Avraham to meet partisans, but for us, who until that moment had only heard rumors about them, this first encounter made an extraordinary impression. Some became so exhilarated that they

46 *Razvedka* is a Russian term meaning a reconnaissance patrol.

started joking that we need to say the *sheheheyanu* blessing.[47] I, for one, wondered how the partisans could ride around so freely everywhere as if there were no Germans in control. A little later, after many encounters with partisans, I stopped wondering.

Leibke the Katzap explained to us that we had now passed through the greatest area of danger. But he warned us that even here, we should remember that the risk of death was lurking at every step of the way. Leibke and Avraham assured us, however, that as much as we wanted to avoid the Germans, the Germans were also afraid of running into partisans and being attacked by them, especially when a small group of Germans had occasion to travel on the roads—they truly trembled at the prospect of a partisan attack. Therefore, they were always heavily armed when they traveled. During our entire journey, until we arrived in the forest, we did not encounter any Germans nor White-Russian police.

For an entire night, we plodded through the muddy fields, taking long detours and avoiding open roads in order not to run into any Germans or policemen. Because of these detours through the fields, our all-night trek only managed to get us 12 kilometers away from Lida. As dawn was breaking, Avraham told us we would soon be entering a large village, where we could rest and get something to eat. He gave us instructions as to how we should behave in the peasants' homes.

Avraham and Leibke told us to spread out among as many houses as possible so that everyone would be able to eat their fill. When I entered a house with several others from our group, the entire peasant family received us with a good morning greeting. They did not wait to be asked, and within moments, a large loaf of reddish bread and a large pitcher of milk were placed on the table. We were certainly hungry, and we attacked that bread and milk, devouring it with great gusto. Within minutes, there was no trace left of either the bread or the milk. During the entire time that we were in the house—even while eating—our guys did not put down their weapons, not even for one second.

47 *Sheheheyanu* is a Jewish blessing recited on special occasions when one wishes to be thankful for a new and unusual experience.

As hungry as I was, I did not get as much pleasure from the bread and milk as I did from observing how the entire peasant family catered to our needs and made every effort to be polite toward us. The only words we heard from them were "dear" and "fine." These very same Christians, who just yesterday had considered us worth no more than worms, these Christians to whom we had humiliated ourselves so that they would do us the great favor of selling us a piece of bread at an exorbitant price, were now suddenly presenting themselves as friends of the Jews when they saw our weapons.

We did not remain in the village for very long. We thanked the peasants for the food and set out once more during daylight hours. The positive impression I got from this first encounter with the peasants stayed with me for a long time, and I felt that I was now entering a new phase of my life. Even though I knew quite well that danger lurked with each step, I was not afraid of anything. And what was so surprising about the fact that we no longer felt fearful? We were only 12 kilometers from Lida and yet there were no Germans anywhere to be seen.

After leaving the village, we walked the entire day without stopping. In the evening, we came to a *hutor* (a single peasant household) and spent the night in a barn. Here, Avraham's group split into two. Those who had weapons remained with Avraham and went off to join the Russian Iskra *otriad*, whereas Leibke the Katzap led the other group to join the Bielski brothers. Most of his group did not have a weapon. I, along with several others from Avraham's group, went with Leibke the Katzap. We still had quite a distance to the Bielski camp—several days of traveling, including detours. This heroic partisan Leibke Orzechovski survived the war and, together with his wife and son, made his home in the United States, where I met with him quite often. He was killed in a car accident in Philadelphia. It was his unfortunate fate that his life ended in such a manner.

After an exhausting two-day march, we arrived at the edge of the forest where the base was located (an area called "the old hute"). Here, we were met by two of Bielski's reconnaissance men on horseback with rifles slung over their shoulders. Their names were Ben-Zion Gulkovitz and Chaim Kravitz. The base was located deep in the forest. It was only at this point that we felt completely drained. However, we did not indulge ourselves with a rest, preferring instead to get to the base as soon as possible. The two scouts led us there.

When we arrived at the base, a panorama of huts spread across a large area of cleared-out forest appeared before us. I observed Jews—men, women, and children—who were not wearing yellow patches and who were smiling and in good spirits. The scene generated an extraordinary first impression on me. I am not ashamed to say that a tear trickled down my cheek at that moment.

From all sides, people started approaching us. Friends and acquaintances threw themselves into our arms. We kissed, embraced, and cried with joy. Another group of over twenty Jews had just torn themselves away from the hands of the murderers. Right away, the Bielski brothers came over to us: Tuvia, Asael, Zusye, and the youngest, Arczyk—the entire leadership.

The commander, Tuvia Bielski, stood out with his tall, broad-shouldered figure. He wore a leather coat and had a revolver at his side—a true commander. From the expression on his face, one could see that he was pleased with the new group of partisans that had just joined, and most importantly, with the newly added weapons, which he immediately began to inspect. He checked the gunlocks to see if they would work when needed. One could also notice a certain disappointment on the faces of several people as some of us didn't have weapons. At that time, the camp already consisted of some 300 people, and weapons were scarce. They eagerly awaited every additional weapon. And, indeed, we soon heard people grumbling in an undertone "another bunch of *malbushim*[48] has arrived." These critical comments were aimed at those who had come empty-handed. I immediately sensed what this implied: those who did not have a weapon were a burden to those who did.

This was not the case, and the *malbushim* subsequently proved their worth through their contribution to and participation in the actions of the Bielski camp in the overall fight against the enemy, particularly during the last phase of the Bielski *otriad*'s existence in the

48 As mentioned earlier, *malbushim* is a derogatory term that was used in the Bielski camp to refer to people who did not have a weapon and were not fighters.

Tuvia Bielski.
Photo Collection, YVA,
4613/183.

Asael Bielski.
Photo Collection, YVA,
4613/184.

Alexander (Zus) Bielski and his wife Sonia.
Photo Collection, YVA, 5674/3.

Naliboki Pushcha.[49] But most importantly, the Bielskis always accepted Jews—with or without weapons, both young and old, anyone who was able to escape from the ghetto and find their way to the camp, even during critical moments for the *otriad*.

They took all of us to a hut, where a doctor examined us. After that, they gave us something to eat. Those who had relatives or close friends in the camp found a place in the family huts. I did not have any friends there. However, I found a family from Lida named Kushelevitz—a husband, wife, and their two sons who were around fourteen and sixteen years old. They took me into their hut, and I stayed with them during the first part of my time in the camp. Kushelevitz had an *obrez*, a rifle with a sawed-off barrel, for the entire family.

49 The Naliboki Pushcha is a large forest complex in the northwestern part of what is now Belarus. The area is full of evergreen forests and large swamps.

CHAPTER FOUR

JOINING THE BIELSKI PARTISANS

The Bielski Brothers

The Bielski family consisted of ten sons and two daughters. The father, David, owned a mill in the village of Stankiewicze, 10 kilometers from the town of Nowogródek in western White Russia. In addition to the mill, he also owned land and worked the fields himself. Raised in the bosom of nature, the Bielskis were very familiar with the forests and fields. They knew all the roads and trails far and wide, and they were also well acquainted with all the peasants in the region, since these peasants would bring grain to their mill.

In December 1941, the Bielski parents perished during one of the German slaughters of the Jews in the area.[50] Tuvia, the oldest brother,

* The first section of this chapter is a short summary of the Bielski *otriad* during its first phase.

50 On December 8, 1941, shortly after the establishment of the Nowogródek ghetto, a brutal *Aktion* took place during which the Bielski parents, David and Beila, were murdered along with approximately 5,000 Jews.

was living in Lida until the German occupation. However, he wanted to be with his family at such a time, and so, risking his life, he set out for home and arrived there safely. Two of the brothers, Zusye and Asael, had managed to flee and hide in the nearby forests. They took knives with them, which were to serve them as weapons in case of danger. They were able to maintain contact with the rest of their family members through peasants with whom they were acquainted. It was not long before the relatives who had managed to save themselves from death joined them. In total, they formed a group of nineteen people. At the time, they had no idea that this small group would grow and transform into a fearsome power against those peasants who collaborated with the Germans to murder Jews, or that it would become a Jewish *otriad* participating in the overall partisan battle against the Nazi enemy.

For two months, they wandered through the forests. During the day, they would warm themselves beside the fires they had built, and at night, they would go to the villages to visit peasant acquaintances to get food, sometimes even spending the night there. But they soon realized that they could not do this for much longer. Eventually, the peasants would get tired of feeding them, and sooner or later, they would be handed over to the Germans. The only solution was to arm themselves. But how and where does one obtain weapons?

They made inquiries as to who of their peasant acquaintances had weapons. Many of the peasants had collected and hidden weapons that had been abandoned by the retreating Soviet soldiers.[51] They contacted these peasants and were able to obtain nine rifles and three revolvers through a combination of cash purchases and trading clothes for weapons. With weapons in hand, they suddenly felt hopeful and secure. Even the peasants were respectful to them.

These events occurred right after the first massacre in the Nowogródek ghetto, where a cousin of theirs named Yudl Bielski still lived. They sent him a letter through a non-Jewish acquaintance of theirs, informing him of their group and then asking him to organize

51 Following the German invasion of the Soviet Union in Operation Barbarossa on June 22, 1941, there was a massive retreat of Red Army soldiers.

a group of Jews and to lead them out of the ghetto.[52] In addition, they told Yudl that the same peasant, Kozlovskiy, who lived in the village of Mokrec, would be waiting to bring the group to the forest. This is exactly what happened. Eight people joined them, and the group grew to twenty-seven people. Now, it was necessary to choose a group leader, and after holding a meeting, it was decided that Tuvia Bielski would be the commander. A decision was also made at this meeting to take revenge on the Nazi murderers, but before anything else, they would eliminate all those peasants who had collaborated with the Germans in murdering the Jews while simultaneously instilling fear in those peasants who still posed a threat to them.

The first act of vengeance was carried out on a family named Marciniewski who lived in the village of Mala Izba (Small Izba). The sons in that family were policemen who had abetted the Nazi occupiers, and they had also taken part in stealing Jewish possessions. Bielski's group broke into their house in the middle of the night, shot everyone, and then set fire to their home. This first act of revenge reverberated throughout every village in the region. Several days later, Bielski's group went to the village of Dula Izba (Great Izba) and carried out a similar act of vengeance with great precision. Shortly after this, they caught a spy who had been lurking around their group. He, too, was shot. These acts of revenge by the Bielski partisans left every peasant in the entire area trembling with fear and meekly complying with everything the Jewish partisans demanded.

Shortly after this, Bielski's group encountered Russian partisans who were operating in that area under the leadership of a Soviet lieutenant named Viktor Panchenkov. On an agreed-upon day, the two groups

52 Koshtzik (Konstantin Kozlovskiy), the Bielskis' non-Jewish acquaintance, slipped into the Nowogródek ghetto with a letter for Yudl in the summer of 1942. The Bielski brothers requested that Yudl organize a group of men, preferably with weapons, to join them in the forest. This Belorussian peasant Koshtzik and his sons Gennadiy and Vladimir worked with the Bielskis to save Jews. Koshtzik was fond of Jews and hated the Germans. His home served as a stopover for Jews who were escaping to the forest. In 1993, Konstantin Kozlovskiy and his sons were awarded the honor of Righteous Among the Nations. See Tec, *Defiance*, pp. 46–47.

assembled in the Buczkowice Forest, where they decided to unite and cooperate with each other. This united *otriad* was called Ordzhonikidze.[53] They also decided then that their first joint operation would be to execute an attack on the Germans and thereby obtain weapons.

This first ambush was carried out in Valevka on the highway between Nowogródek and Nowojelnia, 10 kilometers from Nowogródek. This ambush resulted in the following: four Germans were killed, two vehicles were destroyed, and trophies consisting of two machine guns, four rifles, and 250 bullets were obtained. Encouraged by this first ambush, they later carried out an attack against a guardhouse in Yatsuki that was guarding the train lines, during which two Germans were killed. They also attacked the guardhouse of the Oshmalev courtyard. During this time, the Bielskis were also sending messengers to Nowogródek and Lida, calling on Jews to flee the ghetto and come to the forest to join their group.

The summer of 1942 passed by quickly. Autumn was approaching and beyond that, a long winter. People began to prepare for winter by building *zemlyankas*[54] and gathering food supplies. Before the first snow covered the ground, people had settled into their new accommodation. The White-Russian police, however, were constantly searching for these *zemlyankas* in the forest, and one time, they even discovered one of the Bielski *zemlyankas*. Luckily they managed to run away, however the group lost five people. This happened in Zabielowo in the middle of winter. Following this attack, they were more careful. They divided into smaller groups and built new *zemlyankas* in a different forest. The second attack on one of the Bielski groups was in Chrapiniewo, not far from Iwje. Eight partisans were killed there, including Tuvia Bielski's wife.[55]

53 The Ordzhonikidze *otriad* was a fighting partisan unit named after Grigoriy Ordzhonikidze, a member of the politburo who had died in 1937. The unit began operation in September 1943 in the Nowogródek area, and its tasks included conducting sabotage operations and ambushes, and mining railroads and roads.

54 *Zemlyanka* is a Russian word meaning dugout. These were large underground "earth houses" that were dug out of the ground and covered with a flat roof made of vegetation for camouflage.

55 On the death of Sonia, Tuvia Bielski's second wife, see Tec, *Defiance*, pp. 99–101.

With spring approaching, all the groups reunited in a forest in the area of "the old hute," and once again, a central base was established. Jews from the Lida ghetto began to arrive there, and it did not take long before the base had over 500 Jews—men, women, and children.

In the Jewish Otriad

I spent my first day in the forest in continuous wonderment. I walked from hut to hut and thought about what rare people we Jews are and how quickly we become accustomed to every situation. This is how it was in the ghetto and now here, too, we had been forced back to primeval times. Take the basic necessity of water, for example. When I saw two dug-out wells for the first time in the forest, I was astonished. Such a well had been dug within just a few short hours of establishing the new base and, with luck, water was found after digging just 2–3 meters deep. All four sides of the hole were then fortified with wood, and the water problem was solved.

I had the same feeling of amazement when I first saw the huts for sleeping that had been erected, which also served as protection from the rain. Using just an axe and a saw, a hut such as this was completed in just a couple of hours. We became so adept at setting up these huts that each time a new base was established, rows of such "tents" were erected within just a few hours, their tops covered with branches like those used on Sukkot.[56] When there was heavy rainfall, we really got soaked through. That is why any time we entered a pine tree forest, we peeled the bark off the trees and used it to cover the roof. Only then were we truly protected from the rain.

Life in the *otriad* went according to clearly specified rules that had been developed by the commander, Tuvia Bielski, and members of his staff. The camp commandant made sure that the regulations were

56 The Jewish holiday Sukkot—the Hebrew word meaning booths or huts—symbolizes the frail huts in which the Israelites lived during their forty years of wandering in the desert after the Exodus from Egypt. The *sukkah*, which is built near the homes, needs to be covered with *sehach*—raw, unfinished vegetable matter.

followed. For example, we were not permitted to ever remove our boots or shoes, even while sleeping, and our weapons and rucksacks always had to be ready at our side.

The location of our base changed quite often. Peasants were constantly wandering through the forests, picking mushrooms or berries, and we never knew if they had been sent as a spy in search of partisans. Our guards were posted throughout the forest area around our camp, and if one of them noticed a suspicious looking peasant, he immediately notified the staff who, after some discussion, would sometimes decide to abandon that base.

Moving to a new base took place at night. With such a large group of several hundred people, we had to move with utmost caution. We seldom traveled on open roads, going mainly on side roads through fields and forests, and more than once, we had to wade across a river, as long as it was not too deep. In order not to endanger the lives of the non-fighters—the elderly men, the women, and the children in our group—we took lengthy detours, which added many extra kilometers to the journey.

During the summer of 1943, we stayed at the base in "the old hute," remaining there longer than any other base in the region. Each day after breakfast, we would participate in military exercises, and we learned how to handle weapons. The forests in this region were small and close to forest villages, so we had to be careful. There was no way we could use real bullets when we were learning how to use weapons.

After completing our military exercises, we took off our shirts to rid them of lice. One can imagine how pathetic this scene must have looked. As we were doing this, there was a lot of joking around—and there was plenty to joke about. Nobody made a big deal about it. Later, after we had moved into the Naliboki Pushcha, we came up with a solution to the lice infestation.[57]

57 The partisans in the forests suffered significantly from a lice infestation, which plagued their bodies due to poor hygienic conditions, the absence of bathing opportunities, and a lack of clean clothing. They resorted to crushing the lice or exposing them to heat to eliminate them. For more on the disinfection facility that helped them solve the lice problem, see "A Sausage Factory, a Bathhouse, and a Hospital" in chapter 6.

Feeding such a large group of people was a very difficult problem in terms of both obtaining the products and bringing them to the base. Even distributing these products equally was a problem and often caused conflicts. Every night, one or two groups were sent out on a food-gathering mission. Such groups usually consisted of ten to twelve armed men who were familiar with all the side roads and villages in the region. These were brave and fearless men who elicited respect from the peasants.

Directives issued by the senior partisan command stipulated from which villages the partisans were permitted to obtain products and what they were and were not allowed to do there, but the partisans did not always adhere to the letter of the law. When one of these groups would arrive in a village, they would first go to the well-to-do peasants to collect food. But how did they know who were the wealthiest peasants? The *otriad* had a contact in every village, usually a poor peasant, who supplied all the necessary information. In this way, we had information about every peasant—how much property he owned, how many horses and cows he had, and so on. Such a peasant was called a *legalshchyk*. We hardly ever took anything from these peasants, and quite often they were rewarded with something after a successful *bambioshka*.[58] The peasants were not at all happy with the way our partisans were appropriating their animals and property. However, they were afraid of the partisans. Some peasants tried to outsmart our people by hiding their goods and animals. But this did not help them. Searches were conducted and if anything was found, these peasants would fare much worse. The food-gathering groups made sure they were back at the base by dawn. The requisitioned animals were immediately slaughtered, cut up, and distributed. Everything was done very quickly since a sudden attack could occur at any moment.

The bread problem in the forest was much more difficult to deal with than any other food problem. Food-gathering missions rarely gathered enough bread from the peasants to allow each person in the base to get a piece of bread. So, we were constantly yearning for a bite of bread. When things were peaceful and calm, that is all we thought

58 A *bambioshka* is a partisan food collection mission.

about, but if there was any kind of disturbance and we had to run away, we would completely forget about eating. More than anything, we were afraid of being captured alive by the Germans. When they captured a partisan—especially a Jewish one—they did the most horrible things to him before finally hanging him. Afterward, they left the corpse hanging in the village for many days. However, the day after such an attack, our hunger would return, and once again, all we could think about was that bite of bread.

As soon as we noticed a group returning to the base with a horse and wagon, we ran to see if they had brought any bread. If there was bread, no one would leave, and a long line would soon form. Those at the front would get a piece of bread, but there was not enough for those toward the back of the line. Well, this would cause envy, hatred, and bad blood. But to whom could we complain?

Those who had weapons and were fighting the enemy were in a better position. When they entered a village, they were always able to get food from one of the peasants. We were happy for them and did not begrudge them at all. We knew perfectly well that they were risking their lives far more than those who remained on the base. More than one lost his life fulfilling his duty.

The central staff of the partisan movement in our area had assigned to the Bielski *otriad* a very small region containing villages from whose peasants we could requisition specified products. The Russian partisans were less concerned about toeing the official line and often stole the peasants' valuables for themselves. There were many instances when the peasants complained to the senior command, saying that the Bielski partisans were the culprits. There was no shortage of trouble for Tuvia Bielski, but he was always able to prove that these were false accusations, and in general, our people were careful not to commit such acts. However, many of the peasants had robbed from the Jews and kept their possessions, so when the Bielski partisans entered the home of a peasant, they would search for Jewish belongings, and if they found something, they would unceremoniously confiscate it.

The peasants also had to supply the Germans with certain quotas of wheat and other products, so the peasants were caught between a hammer and an anvil. But, compared to others, the peasants did not suffer as much during the war. They could remain in their own houses, and there was no shortage of food for them and their families. However, they often expressed their disgruntlement toward the Jewish partisans, and only the fear of weapons and acts of revenge forced them to keep their open hatred in check.

In March 1943, ten men were sent out on a food-gathering mission. The leader of this group was a young man from Nowogródek called Abraham Polonski. After the group had completed its task and were on their way back to the base, they stopped at a *hutor* just 5 kilometers from Nowogródek. There, a peasant called Belorus and his family, who knew Polonski well, welcomed the partisans and served them food and drinks. They were tired, so after eating, they lay down for a short rest. That was when Belorus sent his son to Nowogródek to inform the Germans that there were Jewish partisans at his place. Despite the fact that there was a partisan guard posted outside, the son was able to slip away unnoticed and ran all the way to Nowogródek.

A large squad of Germans and White-Russian police soon arrived. They surrounded the house, and nine of our comrades were shot on the spot. During this frightening situation, Polonski was somehow able to crawl into a chicken coop under the oven to save himself. He lay there until the police left, at which point he crawled out from under the stove. We found out later that he shouted at Belorus, saying that for this act of betrayal, revenge would be taken. Belorus's son then shattered Polonski's skull with an axe before he had a chance to respond.

Several days passed, but Polonski and his group did not return. The commander dispatched a reconnaissance patrol to the area where the group had been sent. When the patrol brought back the tragic news, a meeting took place at headquarters immediately. Such treachery could not be allowed to pass without appropriate reprisal. To carry out this punishment, the commander selected a group of twenty-five brave youths, headed by his brother Asael.

One night, our men showed up at the *hutor*. They surrounded the house and knocked on the door. When Belorus opened the door and saw Bielski's men, he knew at once that this was the end for him. Within minutes, no one in his family was still breathing. Afterward, they uttered the blessing *Borei me'orei ha'esh*[59] over the informer's house and its possessions. Tuvia Bielski had instructed them to take nothing. Everything was to be destroyed by fire, including their despicable bodies. One of the men, however, exchanged his old coat for a better coat in the *hutor*. When he put his hand into the pocket, he found a letter that the regional commissar of Nowogródek, Wilhelm Traub, had written to Belorus, thanking him for his loyalty to the German regime and with the hope that all his neighbors would follow his example.

Before they left, the group left a note. It was a warning to all those who collaborated with the German occupiers. This act of revenge elicited the desired response and cast fear over the peasants in the entire region. As a result of this, the Germans set a price of 100,000 rubles on Tuvia Bielski's head.

Killed in an Uneven Battle

The Bielski *otriad* became a place of refuge—with no exceptions—for anyone who succeeded in escaping from the nearby ghettos. Four weeks after I arrived in the forest, the camp had already increased to 600 Jews—men, women, and children. For such a large group of people, it was necessary to send out more groups every night on food-gathering missions, and with each passing day, it became more and more difficult to gather the necessary supplies.

The Russian partisans strongly disapproved of Bielski because he had so many unarmed men and women for whom he had to supply food. They felt that this imposed a burden on them. On two occasions during this time, I was assigned to a group that was sent to the villages to get food. This gave me the opportunity to comprehend the depth of undisguised hostility that the Russian and White-Russian partisans displayed toward the Bielski partisans. The very people with whom

59 The Hebrew *borei me'orei ha'esh* (the Creator of the lights of fire) is referring to God. The phrase is part of a blessing over the flame of a candle that is said by observant Jews at the end of the Sabbath. This is the author's way of saying that the house was burned down.

we fought side by side against the common enemy also endangered our lives.

Among Tuvia's close associates were also those who tried to exert pressure on him not to accept so many people. Their concern was that such a flood of unarmed men, women, and children could, God forbid, bring disaster upon the camp. They also expressed another reason: there would not be enough food for more people. Tuvia Bielski, however, did not allow himself to be influenced by anyone, and he answered them good-naturedly: "Why are you so worried about food? Let the peasants worry. We will take as much food from them as we need, and we just want more Jews to come."

Meanwhile, there were two young Jews from the ghetto who worked in the military hospital in Lida. Bielski's agents established contact with them and helped them "liberate" a large quantity of various medications before fleeing into the forest themselves. Now we had the necessary medicines on our base. In a similar way, we brought in a dentist from Lida with a drill and all her instruments. We brought in a radio with batteries from Lida too.

We stayed at the base in "the old hute" for six weeks. One day, both the reconnaissance patrols and the sentries posted at the forest borders detected suspicious movement in the area near the forest. That night, we abandoned the base and relocated to a forest near Zhuravelnik (Zhuravel'niki). By this point, 100 more people had joined us, so we were now a large group numbering over 700. Here, we experienced a surprise attack by the Germans and White-Russian police, during which ten of our men and women were killed.

Originally, we had chosen this location to be our base for just a few days, since this forest was close to some villages as well as to the main road that was constantly being used by German military vehicles. These were not good qualities for a base, but since we were unsuccessful in finding another "good" forest, we had to stay there for a longer period. We were given strict orders to speak quietly and not to light any bonfires in the evenings.

At night, groups went out on food-gathering missions and returned safely at dawn. In the morning, the goods that had been brought back were distributed. In this way, the days stretched out, one day after another, until two weeks had passed. During this time, our situation improved when we managed to obtain some horses and wagons to use for the food expeditions, the reconnaissance patrols, and the commanders.

One night in May 1943, I was standing watch on one of the narrow roads about half a kilometer from the base. Four shots suddenly shattered the still of the night. This was the signal that there was danger ahead. The alarm sounded from the base to be prepared. The reconnaissance patrols took off in the direction of the *sekret* (partisan guard post) from where the four warning shots had come. A short while later, one of the reconnaissance men returned to the base, and as he ran past me, he yelled, "Be ready!"

I waited, but no one came to relieve me from my post. I did not dare move from my spot without an order. But when I saw our people leaving the forest, I ran toward the base and came across one of our commanders who showed me in which direction to run. At that very moment, I remembered my rucksack! Without considering the danger, I dashed back to the base, ran over to my hut, grabbed my rucksack, and ran back with all the strength I had. I came within a hairsbreadth of losing my life for that rucksack in which I had three pairs of underwear that I had brought with me from the ghetto.

Even before I had rushed into the forest, fearsome gunfire had erupted. I was disoriented for a moment and couldn't figure out exactly where the bullets were coming from and in which direction to run to avoid the enemy. The commander gathered all the armed fighters and led them out to the edge of the forest to return fire. He ordered the rest of the 700 people—especially the elderly men, the women, and the children—to spread themselves out in small groups throughout the forest in order to minimize the number of victims in case of an artillery bombardment.

The two-sided gunfire went on for a long time. The whistling of the bullets echoed throughout the forest and caused great fear. As we later found out, the Germans retreated because they thought that we were a powerful group, and the shooting slowly quieted down. In small groups, we quickly moved from this forest to another forest to distance ourselves from the scene of the raid.

The result of this attack was very painful. Ten people were killed. One could say that we got off with relatively moderate losses. Were it not for the four brave youths who had remained at their posts near the main road, there would have been many more victims. From their hiding place, they had spotted the Germans and the police surrounding our base, so they sounded four shots to warn us. This revealed their position, and they took the first fire from the oncoming Germans, falling in an uneven battle.

One of our partisans, Lipa, did not manage to flee. From afar, he observed the Germans occupying our base, so he quickly climbed up a tall tree and stayed there while the Germans removed everything from the base and burned all the huts. He was within a hairsbreadth of being noticed and therefore being captured alive. However, the Germans took the horses and wagons that we had only recently acquired as well as the two cows that we had just slaughtered. Our radio apparatus and the dental equipment—including a drill—also fell into their hands.

In all the commotion, many did not manage to take their rucksacks, which contained the most necessary items. They were suddenly left with just the clothes they were wearing, without even another shirt. It was at this point when my rescued rucksack turned out to be useful, not only to me but also to several others with whom I shared my three pairs of underwear.

"To Spite the Goyim"*

It took several days after the attack in Zhuravelnik for all the groups who had fled in different directions to reunite and set up a new base in the Jasinowo Forest. It was at this base where the Bielski camp suffered a painful experience that revealed the ugly antisemitic face of the senior leadership of the Russian partisans.

* The word *goyim*—usually referring to non-Jews in general but in this context referring to other *otriads* in the forest—has been used here to keep the spirit of the original Yiddish. It refers to the author's recollection of Tuvia Bielski's speech in which he reassured his Jewish partisans that their *otriad* will succeed despite the negative actions of others toward them.

As mentioned earlier, Tuvia Bielski had established a partnership with a Russian lieutenant, Viktor Panchenkov, and for a while, they operated together under the name of the Ordzhonikidze *otriad*. Later, Tuvia was confronted with a hostile attitude from this very same Viktor Panchenkov as well as from other Russian commanders. Suddenly, they started to look for faults with the Bielski camp. Apparently, it irritated them that the Bielskis were gathering defenseless Jews—both men and women—however, the driving force behind this was clearly a good deal of antisemitism. For them, the Jewish camp was a thorn in their side, and they were looking for excuses to push Bielski out of the partisan region.

Indeed, it did not take long. One day, Viktor and several Russians from the senior partisan command came to Tuvia and informed him that only armed fighters would be allowed to remain in the region from now on. Everyone else—unarmed men, women, and children—had to go to the Naliboki Pushcha, the large forest complex in Western Belorussia. Initially, this news was very distressing for Tuvia, and it pained him deeply. After experiencing so much trouble and danger, the *otriad* had finally managed to obtain a small number of weapons, and now Tuvia's supposedly good friend was taking away most of the weapons together with the best fighters in the camp. However, there was nothing he could do about it. The power was with the Russians.

The Russians told us to line up, and they chose around eighty of the best armed men to be assigned to Viktor's group. Tuvia's brother Zusye, who had been with his brothers the entire time, was one of the partisans selected to join Viktor's group. Viktor appointed him to be the commander of a group of horsemen, and he went with them and remained there until the liberation. About ten of those who had been chosen, however, decided to remain with Tuvia, and right there on the spot, they parted from Viktor because they did not want to leave their brothers and sisters. The two machine guns also remained with Bielski.

After Tuvia had recovered from the shock, he called out to his people: "Friends, do not worry, we will find other weapons, even more than we had. The *otriad* will grow with more Jews—to spite the *goyim*. Don't worry. I am going with you. We will show them what Jews can accomplish." I am sure that at the time, Tuvia Bielski had no inkling that his words would, in fact, one day be realized, and that his *otriad* would become known throughout the length and breadth of the partisan region for important accomplishments that proved useful not only to his own large *otriad* but also to many Russian *otriads* operating in the Pushcha region.

Right after the selected Jewish partisans went with Viktor, Tuvia began to prepare the *otriad* to leave. He held a meeting with his staff during which a plan was developed for the move to the Naliboki Pushcha. The most important thing to do was to prepare a supply of food to take with us that would be sufficient for the initial period. We knew that getting food in the Pushcha would be much more difficult than in our current location. Here, the villages were close to the forest, and carrying out a food-gathering operation at night was one of the easiest things to do, but there, the forest was surrounded by swamps and deep mud. The roads were very bad, making it very difficult to travel with a horse and wagon. At the meeting, it was decided that many more groups would be sent out to gather food.

After the attack, we no longer had any horses or wagons, so we had to carry out new theft operations. For three weeks, two or three groups were sent out every night to various villages to carry out *bambioshkas*. Before, we would borrow a horse and wagon from a peasant—which was returned to him after unloading the food at the base—whereas now, with every appropriation, we also took the horse and wagon together with the goods. During those few weeks, we were able to amass a huge supply of all sorts of food. Every group returned with a horse and wagon filled with food, and tied to the back of the wagon were a couple of cows. Even calves were not rejected, and room was somehow found in the wagon for them.

The distance to the Naliboki Pushcha was more than 100 kilometers, but since we had to use side roads, the actual travel distance amounted to much more. Aside from that, we had to cross the Niemen and the Berezina Rivers. As we were beginning to leave the base, I caught a glimpse of the panorama of our camp as far as the eye could see, and I thought to myself that this is probably what the Exodus from Egypt must have looked like. Seven hundred Jews, among them a large number of elderly men, women, and young children, setting out on an unfamiliar journey, where with every step lurked the danger of encountering the Germans and White-Russian police. But no matter how strange it may seem, we were not afraid. Under the protection of our commander Tuvia Bielski, his brother Asael, and the twenty or so armed men, we felt safe.

After a long march, we reached the Niemen River. The Russian partisan *otriads* had their own private ferry at the Niemen. They would pull it onto the shore after they had finished using it so that the Germans would not capture it. I don't remember if we used this ferry or another one. But this crossing—involving so many people as well as tens of horses, wagons, and cows—took an entire day. Boarding the ferry was done in an orderly way under the direction of our commander and the armed men.

Tired after many days and nights of traveling, we finally arrived at the Berezina River, where we encountered a difficult situation. There was no ferry here, and we had to turn to the peasants for help. After much trouble, we finally found a couple of peasants with boats. We only had these few boats to transfer our large group. It was a nice bit of luck that the river was shallow enough in that spot to enable the horses and wagons to cross over in the water. Here, too, crossing the river took the entire day and late into the night.

It was our fate to experience a tragic incident when we lost a young boy. The peasants who owned the boats told us that, from time to time, the Germans and the police would come to this spot. Upon hearing this, people became a little nervous, and everyone wanted to reach the other side as quickly as possible. Standing near me was a young boy and his sister. I think they were from Lida. The brother did not want to wait for his turn in the line and began to swim across the river. When he had almost reached the other side, he ran out of strength and drowned. His sister had warned him not to go into the water, but he didn't listen to her. She was shattered by this tragedy, and we could not console her.

When we were finally on the other side, we were able to breathe more freely. By this time, we were in the vicinity of the Pushcha, which meant that the danger of encountering Germans and the police was lower. This, however, was nothing more than an illusion.

In the Naliboki Wilderness

The Naliboki Forests cover an area of 400 square kilometers. During the 1930s, the forests belonged to the well-known Vilna forest merchants, the Solomyanski brothers. When the antisemitic policies began with the purpose of forcing the Jews out of their long-established economic positions, the Polish government—through various edicts—simply stole their possessions. When the partisan movement in western White Russia began to develop and the smaller forests had become crowded, the Naliboki Pushcha became the main location for tens of *otriads* and brigades. They were under the control of a central headquarters, with the Russian General Platon as the commander.[60]

The moment we first set foot on the soil of the Naliboki Pushcha, the atmosphere was completely different. We felt a new kind of security, as if we were in our own partisan kingdom, and people soon began to sing. Before long, the singing echoed and resounded far and wide throughout the forests. All songs were acceptable, whatever a person knew was accepted—a Russian song or a Jewish folksong. They wanted to make up for all that time in the small forests where singing was not permitted and even talking had to be done quietly. The summer of 1943 had just begun, and we also felt like it was summer in our souls. We had survived so many dangers, but we were now among Jews in the forest, and the feeling that we were more secure here elevated our mood. We forgot about our tiredness.

We set up our first base by the banks of Kromań Lake, several tens of kilometers from the town of Naliboki. Here, people had a craving to build themselves more comfortable huts. After all, there was no shortage of trees, and it seemed that we would be staying here for the entire summer, no longer having to constantly change our base. We also had to erect a rain cover to protect the goods we had brought with us. In short, our plan was to stay here until winter. How could we have known that three weeks later we would have to flee, and in such a way that we had never done before.

60 General Vasily Yefimovich Chernyshev, codenamed General Platon (1908–1969), was a Soviet partisan commander.

Alongside our arrival in the Pushcha, a totally different way of feeding the camp was established. Since obtaining food was very difficult, we had to be very rigorous and efficient with the food we had. The commander decided to set up one main kitchen for the entire *otriad*, similar to other partisan *otriads* that were located in the Pushcha. In a nearby village, we found two large iron pots that the Soviet army had probably left behind following their retreat. The commander ordered them to be taken.

Now it was necessary to have a cook. The commander was soon made aware that I had been the cook in the Lida ghetto kitchen, so he summoned me and appointed me to be the cook in the main kitchen, a role that I accepted and felt good about, even though I knew that it would not be an easy task in these primitive forest conditions. However, I felt fortunate to be able to contribute in some capacity to the *otriad*, and if I could do this as a cook, I was certainly on board with it, regardless of how difficult the work might be. And most unexpectedly, I became "popular" in the *otriad*, just like when I became the cook in the ghetto kitchen in Lida. From that very first day, everyone was already calling me by my name, whereas before it was mostly the Lida people who knew me. I was chief cook until the very last day, until the liberation.

This is what my work was like. The pots we had taken hung from chains between two trees, and under them was a fire. A thick smoke would envelope me, causing my eyes to water, but I could not back away from the pots, not even for a moment, because I had to keep stirring them continuously with a large paddle to make sure that the food would not stick to the bottom and burn. The people standing around and watching me marveled at how I could continue to stand there and endure the hellish fire and suffocating smoke. Yes, it's true that my eyes would burn bitterly from the smoke, and the sweat would pour from me like a river, but in spite of that, it was much easier for me to tolerate this work than the work in the kitchen in the Lida ghetto, since I was not under the supervision of that antisemitic woman.

I had to cook and then distribute the food three times a day. Of course, I had plenty of helpers. Handing out the food was actually the most thankless job of all. People could barely wait for their portion of soup, which consisted of pieces of meat, barley, and potatoes. If there was no barley, we made do with wheat. Everyone was anxious to receive a good portion to still their hunger until the next meal. As for bread, one could only dream of that. While standing in line for their soup, the people would plead: "Nu Lazar, dive down." They wanted me to dig deeper into the pot. At that time, we actually suffered from hunger quite a bit. But our lives felt more secure, which compensated for everything else. We also expected Asael Bielski to arrive any day with a large shipment of food: with this delivery, our future food situation would improve.

During those long summer days, both men and women were busy with various tasks by the huts, at the sentry posts, and in the kitchen, but at the same time, all they could think about was their anticipated portion of soup. The scent of the pine trees and the fresh forest air increased our appetite even more. But when night fell, we felt the significance of being in the Pushcha, and the entire camp was transformed into a singing festival. People from neighboring huts sat in a circle, lit a fire using dried twigs, and began to sing. At night, the pine trees literally intoxicated us, the fires lit up the entire area, and human shadows moved around from one circle of singers to another. What didn't we sing? We even sang operatic arias.

There, I became friendly with a fellow Vilnaite Solomon Taub, who was there with his wife and sixteen-year-old daughter, as well as with Hershel Feldman and his wife Ida, who had lived in the Lida ghetto in the same place I had lived—in Henech the Yellow's courtyard—and so we were already somewhat acquainted. Hershel Feldman and Taub's wife sang duets together from various classical operas. I also had some familiarity with classical music. Nu, on nights such as those, we had no desire to go to sleep and, of course, on such nights we forgot about eating. Who could have known that this joyful, life-loving, and genteel Hershel would later fall in battle with the enemy? He was assigned to the mine group, and during one of the missions to blow up the train lines, he was killed.[61] And during those nights, who could have known

61 Hershel Feldman was born in 1910 in Dereczyn and moved to Lida after he got married. He escaped to the forests and excelled in mines and sabotage. He was killed during a mission to ambush a convoy of German cars in the winter of 1943.

that this idyllic period would only last a short time and that even here we would have to suffer hellish experiences?

A couple of weeks after settling into life in the Pushcha, Asael Bielski and his group arrived, bringing thirty wagons filled with food as well as many cows and horses. The mood lightened, and everyone saw that there was no reason to worry about going hungry. Soon, more groups were preparing to go on food-gathering missions. However, at the same time, fear of an attack caused a nagging sense of uneasiness to grow in the *otriad*. There were people with us who had been in the Lipiczanska Pushcha the previous summer and had lived through one of the worst attacks on the partisans of that period. When they spoke of that attack, they scared us. We were worried that such an attack would be repeated in the Naliboki Pushcha. The Germans knew that there were thousands of well-organized partisans in the Naliboki Pushcha who were causing them great trouble on both the train lines and the roads that led to the front, and they therefore conducted major attacks against the partisans like they had done the previous summer.

Furthermore, the traitorous Russians and Ukrainians along with the Soviet General Vlasov[62] had surrendered to the Germans, and they united with the Lithuanians, Latvians, and Estonians. They were armed with all sorts of weapons—tanks, explosives, and artillery—and under the leadership of German military personnel, they were sent to wipe out the partisans, who were unable to take on such a powerful force in open combat and would, therefore, pull back. The Pushcha, however, contained hazardous sections covered with swamps, so they retreated there. Only if the partisans found themselves surrounded did they stand and fight to the very last bullet, which would be saved for themselves so as not to be captured alive by the enemy.

Tens of Soviet *otriads* were spread throughout the Naliboki Pushcha. Sentry posts were set up along every road, watching for any strangers that entered the forest. The central headquarters were also located there, with General Platon in command. All orders to the

killed during a mission to ambush a convoy of German cars in the winter of 1943.

62 Andrey Vlasov (1901–1946) was a Soviet Red Army general and collaborator with Nazi Germany.

various partisan units in the region were issued from these headquarters, and it was also where the password for all the *otriads* was established. If someone did not know the password when encountering a partisan combat unit on one of the partisan roads, he was immediately disarmed and often shot on the spot. In addition, one needed written permission from one of the senior staff officers to move around in the Pushcha. It was not unusual for a peasant to enter the Pushcha and never return home. It was not easy to ascertain whether such a peasant was a German spy, so they did not stand on ceremony and made short work of him.

Barely a week had passed since Asael Bielski and his group had brought the large shipment of food, when our reconnaissance men came back with the alarming news that the Germans were preparing a massive attack on the Naliboki Pushcha. We did not panic at this news. After all, we had already survived several attacks and had suffered relatively few casualties. There were also tens of thousands of partisans in the Pushcha under the central command, so our commander Bielski and his chief of staff Lazar Malbin[63] would certainly be in contact with central headquarters. And, indeed, that is what happened.

Of course, during those first few days, not everyone knew exactly what was going on. However, one only had to look at the worried faces of the commander and his aides to immediately understand that the situation was dire. Our reconnaissance men were constantly riding their horses back and forth between the base and central headquarters. A few days later, we all knew that we were about to face a severe test.

After returning from a meeting with General Platon, the commander assembled everyone in the camp and informed us that 100 men were to go immediately to help cut down trees and lay them across the roads near the forest to hinder the enemy's movements. General Platon demanded that a group of armed partisans be placed under the command of his staff.

Michal Mechlis and Akiva Szymonowicz were two friends in our *otriad*. Mechlis was a teacher by profession, but for a certain period of

63 Lazar Malbin (1903–1989) lived in the Nowogródek ghetto with his wife and children, who perished in the ghetto *Aktion* in the summer of 1942. He escaped to the forests, met Bielski, and was appointed chief of staff in the *otriad*.

time, he had worked for the owners of a large forest and was therefore well acquainted with every inch of the Pushcha. Akiva, who had been a merchant, was also very familiar with the vast forest region. In short, the two of them were now the most important people in the *otriad*, and the commander would meet with them constantly. It soon became clear that we were surrounded on all sides. The only way out was through the forest swamps, and we hoped that the enemy would have no desire to slog through the swamps. With lightning speed, we transferred our base close to the swampy forest areas.

It just so happened that at this time, the *otriad* had accumulated a sizable supply of food as well as fifty cows, which provided milk for the children and weak individuals. We had also amassed the same number of horses and wagons with all sorts of additional equipment as well as over 500 pood[64] of various grains. Obtaining this material and bringing it into the forest—hauling it over the muddy roads and across the Niemen and Berezina Rivers—had involved tremendous effort and great risk. Now, we would have to leave all our stock behind.

But for now, we loaded our belongings onto wagons and moved to another base near the swamps. We stayed at this new base for another two weeks during which our reconnaissance people maintained constant contact with the other *otriads* in the Pushcha. Early one morning, they issued an alert: a large enemy armed force was approaching. We even heard the rumble of tanks.

64 Pood is a Russian unit of weight equal to approximately 16 kilograms.

CHAPTER FIVE

OUR SPLINTERED PARTISAN CAMP

The Retreat to the Swamps

That morning, the commander issued an order for us to leave everything behind and march into the swamps. At the front were men carrying small children on their shoulders. Behind them were the elderly and the women who were watching over the older children, and at the back of the column was the commander and a group of armed men. At the start of the march, the commander mounted his horse along with his aides. Of course, we envied them because they did not have to wade through the swampy waters. However, after several tens of meters, trudging along step by step, the horses declared a strike and refused to go any further, as if they were saying, "Do something about it!" The riders dismounted, abandoned the horses, and continued with us on foot.

As we were leaving the base, there were people who took some of the wheat kernels that were in the sacks on the wagons and poured them into their rucksacks and pockets. The freshly slaughtered cows were hanging on trees, and there were some who sliced off a hunk of meat to take with them in the hope of being able to cook it; however, they soon discarded it.

We had barely managed to travel a few hundred meters when night fell. Traveling through the mud in the dark was dangerous, so the commander ordered us to remain where we were overnight. Each person picked out either a tree or a low-hanging branch to lean against. The night passed in this way, and as soon as there was a glimmer of light, we resumed our journey, dragging ourselves onward.

It was a remarkable scene seeing the entire camp stretched out one behind the other, wading through the swamps, 700 people, among them a large number of women, young children, and those who were sick and frail. In some places, when you took a step with one foot, you could barely pull out the other one. Younger people had an easier time of it, but it was much more difficult for the older men and women. The men continued to carry the smaller children on their shoulders, lifting them onto their heads in the deepest parts. When someone no longer had the strength to carry a child, another man would take over. They also helped the elderly people when someone got stuck in a deep spot.

While we were moving through the swampy forests, we were able to tolerate the difficulties since we could at least grab onto a tree and rest a little. But our hearts sank when the forest ended, and all we saw ahead was the long, extensive, swampy fields, overgrown with tall grass. These fields stretched out before us for many, many kilometers. This is what we would have to cross. Our thinking was that once we had passed these swamps, we would be safer, as the enemy would not chase us any further than the swamps.

One behind the other, we began to trudge through the swampy fields. We couldn't even feel the wetness and the fatigue while we were constantly searching the skies to see if any enemy planes were flying above. What would have happened to us had just one plane noticed us in the open field? None of us would have come out of there alive. This was truly a miracle. For the entire day, we were immersed in this mud until we finally reached a dry forest. Another miracle was that no one was left behind in the swamps.

It was already night when we reached this dry forest. Drenched right through and with our strength completely drained, we collapsed on the ground and slept for the rest of the night. However, in the morning, we were woken by a heavy barrage of cannon fire. Mine-throwers and airplanes were battering the forest with bombs. We were left with no alternative but to continue to hide in the thick, dark forest, without showing any signs of life. We were ordered not to move and to remain sitting quietly beneath the trees in silence.

Our clothes were soaked so we removed them one at a time and laid them on the grass to dry out. Some had lost their shoes in the swamps and were now barefoot. No one was too upset about this, though. The most important thing was that our heads were still on our shoulders. Once we had somewhat recovered, we put on our dry clothes and found a dense, dry forest to hide beneath the trees.

During those first couple of days, we did not even think about eating. But by the third day, hunger hit us hard, so we took advantage of the short periods between airplane attacks to gather blackberries, strawberries, and mushrooms, which were plentiful there. To some extent, this stilled our hunger. However, our biggest worry was the little children. We did everything we could to ensure that the children would not go hungry. Those who had taken the wheat kernels upon our hasty departure gave them to the women to make some cereal in a tin over a small fire to ease their hunger. Some people had tobacco, and this was truly a treasure. When someone rolled a cigarette, at least ten people would take a puff.

The days dragged on and felt like years. Partisans from other *otriads* who had managed to break through the encirclement began to arrive, and they gave us information about the progress of the enemy attack. Some of the *otriads* had engaged the enemy in open battle, and many partisans had been killed. We remained in that forest for six days. However, staying in the forest meant certain death by starvation. Our only alternative was to break through the blockade.

For this we depended on Mechlis and Akiva. Our hopes were pinned on them to get us out of our predicament. They took on the roles of being our "Moshe" and "Aaron."[65] In short, Mechlis and Akiva, escorted by several armed men, went off to find a way to break through the blockade. I do not know what this group of "spies" experienced during their mission, but it resulted in a favorable outcome for our camp, and they returned with good news for the commander. They had found a way out via a canal leading to the Berezina River, which would allow us to emerge from the Pushcha.

The commander decided that the camp should be divided into smaller groups. Every hour, one of these groups left the camp. Each group was assigned a commander and was accompanied by several armed men. Both a location within the Nowogródek Forest and a date were set for all the groups to reunite after the attack was over. The commander Tuvia Bielski and his aides waited until all the groups had left, and I ended up in the last group with the commander. Despite the fact that we were extremely weak after six days without food, we walked the 25 kilometers to the Berezina River in just five hours. A better description is that we didn't really walk but rather were carried along by the momentum.

It was already dark by the time we reached the first village, so the commander decided that we should remain there overnight. We entered the houses, planning to end our hunger after our long fast. Most of the peasants in this village, however, were poor, and it was just my bad luck that I didn't even get a crumb of bread. So, I sated my thirst with a long drink of water and immediately settled myself into a corner and fell asleep. Early the next morning, we resumed our march along the back roads and trails. I was very happy to be part of the commander's group, which had a significant number of armed men. Being with them made me feel as if I also had a weapon. But the devil interfered, and I suddenly got separated from the group and had to deal with a whole new bundle of trouble.

After having walked a long stretch past the Berezina River, we entered a village to get something to eat. This was a very large village, so we scattered ourselves among the houses, several people to each house. A young man and I ended up in a house that was located at

65 This is referring to the biblical tale of the Exodus of the Israelites from Egypt.

the very edge of the village, and we were hosted by some very nice peasants. They quickly placed a loaf of pink bread and a tin pitcher of milk on the table. It had been weeks since we had seen any bread, and here was an entire loaf! We quickly finished half the loaf and the entire pitcher of milk and took the other half with us. We thanked the peasant for his hospitality, left the village, and waited for the rest of the group. After a while, we wondered why we had not seen anyone. We soon, however, found out the bad news: everybody had already left.

We went to the nearby forest, thinking that they would be there. After traveling somewhat deeper into the forest, we met a shepherd feeding his animals. We asked him if he had seen any partisans passing through. Instead of answering our question, he told us that just a short while earlier, cars carrying Germans had driven by. Now we understood why our people had left in such a hurry.

In the meantime, it was just the two of us. At least I was lucky that my brother-in-misery had a rifle. Until we found our people, I was happy to not feel so abandoned or at the mercy of the whims of fate. We didn't know which way to go, but it was clear to us that before anything else, we needed to reach the other side of the Niemen River. We figured that we would then find out if our partisans had passed through the villages there. We began to wander through the forest, not knowing if we were walking in the right direction to the Niemen.

As we were roaming through the forest, we ran into some peasants. They were fussing over a primitive still they were using to brew liquor. Right away, they welcomed us with some of their "product" and told us that we could drink as much as we wanted. However, we understood that their ulterior motive was to get us drunk and steal our rifle. Just to be polite, we drank a little. It was forbidden to get drunk, especially when we were on the road, but only a rare person could resist such a temptation when coming across a peasant with moonshine. More than one partisan had ignored this prohibition and had lost his life because of liquor.

We took one of the peasants with us, and he showed us the way to the Niemen River. It took a very long time before a boat took us to the other side. In a village right by the river, we found out that many of our people had passed through. We were now certain that we would eventually reunite with the rest of the group.

Alone among Our Own Hooligans

After breaking through the German blockade in the Naliboki Pushcha, the splintered partisan groups had found a hiding place in this new region, and it became crowded there. For a while, contact with central headquarters had been severed, so the groups did not know anything about each other's whereabouts. In addition, almost all those who had survived the attack were left half-naked. Some had torn boots, while others had no boots at all. People were literally walking around barefoot.

The Russian and White-Russian partisans began to look for opportunities to snatch an undamaged pair of pants, a jacket, or boots. There were many thugs among them who were fanatical antisemites. Before the attack, there had been discipline in their *otriads*, and antisemitism was explicitly forbidden. They had been afraid to show their hatred toward Jews. But after the attack, they no longer had any commanders in charge of them, and they felt free to act as they pleased.

This was the start of a new set of troubles for the Bielski partisans. These loathsome hooligans took advantage of the fact that the Bielski Jewish *otriad* had splintered into smaller groups and were not well armed. The thugs would attack these small groups of Jewish partisans, who had no idea that they had to be wary of their own comrades. They took the Jews' weapons and even removed the boots from their feet. If someone was wearing a decent article of clothing, they took that as well. More than one Jew paid with his life for trying to resist. This was a bitter pill to swallow after the attack, whose impact everyone still felt deep in their bones. But even worse was the moral pain. Just yesterday, we were all united, in a manner of speaking—comrades with the same troubles. We had defended ourselves against the common enemy and together had escaped the attack. But they had suddenly transformed into ordinary thieves and had become our enemies. Now, we had to be wary of them in exactly the same way we had to be wary of the White-Russian police and the Germans.

However, when a group of Russian partisans once encountered a group of our youths, the Jews were not scared. In a turnaround, the thugs were taught a lesson when the Jews actually seized the Russians' weapons, and the thugs then begged the Jews to give them back. They knew quite well that it would be all over for them if they returned to their *otriad* without their weapons.

My companion and I had the misfortune of encountering some of these hooligans. As we were leaving the first village near the Niemen River, we came face-to-face with ten Russian partisans. At this point, we knew nothing about the danger from such a group, so we approached them and greeted them in a very friendly manner to inquire about our fellow partisans. Before we could even utter a word, they grabbed my companion's rifle, threw him down, and then started to strip him of his boots and his pants, which were both in good condition. At first, he tried to defend himself, but then they threatened to shoot him. The life of a Jewish partisan meant nothing to them. What could we possibly do with just one rifle against a large armed band? One of the Russians actually did my companion a favor by throwing his own pair of torn pants at him. I had better luck. My clothes and shoes had become so tattered in the swamps that they weren't worth stealing.

We soon got a taste of how it feels to enter a peasant's house without a rifle. Instead of ordering the peasant to give us something to eat, we had to beg. And we had to go to several houses in the village before we were able to get something to eat. The peasants questioned us about our lack of weapons. What kind of partisans were we without weapons? We had one explanation for them: During the attack, our rifles had been damaged in the swamp waters. After all, we could not tell them that other partisans had taken the weapons from us. They would have ridiculed us—and rightly so.

One time, my companion went into a peasant's house to ask for bread and was in there for a long time. I was waiting for him on the road near the village. Seeing in the distance Russian partisans approaching—with whom I had no desire to encounter—I quickly took off in the opposite direction. I was left alone. My rucksack, which contained all my necessities, had not yet completely dried out from the soaking it had received in the swamps and was now at risk. In it was a change of clothes, a razor, and a few other small items. The Russian bandits would have certainly taken these things.

It turned out that I did not have to wander around alone for very long. I met a small group of comrades from our camp, and I joined them. There were fifteen people in the group, but only eight of them had rifles. We chose a suitable spot in a forest near Zhuravelnik and settled there. At night, we would go to the villages to take food from the peasants. Whoever's turn it was to go to the villages received one of the eight rifles. There was no shortage of food then, and we no longer had to yearn for bread. Slowly, over time, more people joined our group—men and women from the Bielski *otriad*—and we now totaled sixty people with twelve rifles.

Once, in the middle of the night, I was standing watch at the edge of the forest near a narrow road. There was a hut not too far from the forest. Suddenly, shooting broke out so near that I thought it had to be close to the forest. My only thought was that the Germans had discovered us. It was dark, so I hid beneath a bush and remained there. Then, I saw the sky turn red, and I realized that the hut was on fire. The shooting did not last long, and I remained hidden for a while longer. When it fell completely quiet, I came out from under the bush and resumed my post.

I sensed that something odd was going on. It was daybreak—already long after the time when someone was supposed to come and take my place on guard duty—and nobody had come to relieve me. I started to suspect that the shooting, which had echoed like thunder throughout the forest, had scared my comrades, causing them to run away, and in their haste, they had forgotten about me. I headed back into the forest. I looked here; I looked there; but no one was around.

When I had gone off that night to my guard post, I had left my rucksack with the two men who were also sleeping under the same tree. I started to search for that tree. But how do you find a specific tree in the forest when they all look alike? I wandered around for many hours searching for my rucksack, but it was hopeless. All I could think of was that they had taken my rucksack with them. In the meantime, I consoled myself with the fact that I still had the rifle from my night on guard duty. I would therefore be able to go to a village and get food without having to beg for a piece of bread. However, at the same time, I was alone and afraid of the hooligan partisans. I lingered in the forest, hoping that one of my comrades would come looking for me, most likely the one to whom the rifle belonged. I waited for a day and a night, but no one came. I was very hungry, so I left the forest.

I didn't know where I was nor where I was going. Wandering through the fields for a while, I came across some shepherds feeding their animals. I asked them about the region and found out about the fire. Four partisans had been sleeping inside a stable near the previously mentioned hut. Apparently, the White-Russian police heard about this, and a large police force came down, surrounded the stable, and ordered the partisans to surrender. The partisans responded with a barrage of fire from their rifles. The police returned fire with a hail of bullets. The shooting set the stable ablaze, and it was burned to a cinder, as were the partisans. One of the policemen, the shepherds told me, had been hit by a bullet and was dragged away covered in blood.

I continued on my way and kept to the side roads near villages, believing that only in this way, sooner or later, I would meet up with our people. And that is exactly what happened. On the third day, I encountered several partisans from my previous group, one of whom was the owner of the rifle. We were both very happy to see each other. His eyes lit up when he saw that I had his rifle in my hands. After returning the rifle to him, my first question was, "Where is my rucksack?"

He responded by telling me about their escape. When the shooting had started, they had, indeed, thought—just as I had—that the Germans had discovered us. In a panic, they began to run every which way. Who could possibly think of grabbing my rucksack at a moment like that? Each one grabbed his own belongings and fled. In this way, the entire group split up, and no one knew the whereabouts of anyone else.

So, I had no choice but to "recite *Kaddish*"[66] for my rucksack. How much effort I had expended rescuing it from the attacks along with my own bones. I had not parted with it even in the deep swamps, dragging it on my back when I could barely drag my own feet. And now, after all this, it was gone because of an unfounded panic. My dismay grew when I realized that I no longer had a shirt to change into nor a razor with which to shave.

66 *Kaddish* is the Jewish mourning prayer. This was his way of saying a final goodbye to the rucksack.

The Splintered Groups of the Bielski Otriad

After our group fell apart at the time of the shooting incident, I ended up joining various small groups that stayed together for a few days before disbanding. Everyone was only thinking of themselves and how they could link up with a well-armed group. Elderly men and women therefore found themselves in a very difficult situation; however, they managed to get enough food in most cases. The village peasants treated the elderly Jews in a considerate manner and did not turn them away hungry from their homes. During this particular time, it even went so far that some—true, just a very few—could no longer bear it and decided to make their way back to the Lida ghetto until the *otriad* would regroup. They said that in the ghetto, they would find some clothing and a pair of intact shoes, and then they would return to the *otriad.*

For around a week, I was with such a group who were discussing a return to the ghetto. Most of the group had come out of the attack literally half-naked and also suffering from various ailments. I remember one of them. Everyone in the forest loved him and treated him with compassion. He suffered from problems with his lungs, but despite this, he was cheerful and had a zest for life. His name was Monik Przepiórka, and he came from Łódź. After the attack, he lost the will to live. Several people from this group, including Przepiórka, decided to return to the ghetto. I advised them against making such a senseless move, but they paid me no heed and left. They actually made it back to the Lida ghetto but later shared the same fate as all those who had remained in the ghettos. Przepiórka, however, had the good luck to escape and was able to return to the Naliboki Pushcha.

Another time, fate brought me together with a small group where no one had any weapons. A person has to eat, after all, but nobody wanted to beg from the peasants and then have to listen to their mocking retorts. One of the members of this group, a young man from Lida, had an idea to outwit the peasants. Using a small pocket knife, he carved out a couple of "revolvers" from a branch. Straps were found and attached to a belt, and the "revolvers" were held in the pockets. With the help of these "revolvers," we took what we needed from the peasants, and then we were no longer hungry.

One evening, as I was sitting with my group in a forest near the Niemen River, sounds of shooting shattered the stillness. We didn't have any weapons—maybe one rifle—so the best thing to do was to get out of there as quickly as possible. We ran down to the river and started to look for a boat to get us to the other side. All of a sudden, Russian partisans, armed from head to foot, showed up and grabbed the boat that had almost been ours. Well, if that had been the only annoyance, it wouldn't have been so bad, but the way they spoke to us irritated us even more.

"You guys are cowards. What kind of partisans are you that you run away from a fight. This little boat wasn't left here for you. Turn around, and go fight the *svolochs*,[67] our enemies." These big heroes expected us to fight the enemy without any weapons.

From the time I got separated from the commander's group and had begun wandering along roads and through forests, I never stopped counting the days until all the splintered groups were supposed to reunite. Only now I finally understood how good it had been when we were under the watchful eye of the commander and his aides.

Just two weeks before the planned reunion, I had the good fortune to join a group of comrades. My experience with them made up for all my troubles until now. The group consisted of twelve people from Lida. Five of them had weapons, and they all knew me. The commander of this group was a young man from Lida named Blacher, who was there with his wife. Later, he became the commander's adjutant. While I was with this group during those last two weeks, I no longer had any problems. We camped in a small forest, and we would go to the peasants and "take" enough food from them to feed all of us every night. I was even able to get a change of clothes and two sheets of thick homespun linen, which I used at night to lay on and to cover myself. This was quite an impressive loot after I had lost my rucksack and had been left with just the clothes on my back.

One day in this forest, I had a thoroughly enjoyable experience. Blacher knew where the commander and his brothers were located, so he went there and brought them to us. Well, we had ourselves quite a

67 *Svolochs* is a Slavic vulgarity that can be interpreted as dirty dogs or swines.

feast that day. We ate well—we demolished a couple of sheep—and even managed to get some liquor (samogon).[68] We made quite the *L'Chaim*,[69] finishing our day with a very pleasurable drinking session.

The commander told us how he had taught a lesson to the partisan-bandits, those who had demonstrated their "bravery" against small and weak Jewish groups. Once again, I thought about my own fate, about what had happened to me, and felt that I would have been spared so much aggravation had I not been separated from the commander and his group. But what can one do in the face of destiny?

At last, the day that everyone had been waiting for so impatiently arrived. I went with Blacher's group into the Jasinowo Forest, and we met up with the commander, his staff, and hundreds of partisans. We stayed in that forest for several weeks and waited for all our people to gather together.

It's important to note at this point that the attack on the partisans also had a fatalistic effect on the Jews in the Lida ghetto. Were it not for the blockade, hundreds more Jews would have certainly joined the Bielskis. The fifty men and women who miraculously escaped the ghetto during its liquidation on September 18, 1943, and later joined the Bielski camp told us what happened. After the people in the Lida ghetto found out that an attack was being mounted against the partisans, they temporarily stopped going into the forest. Moreover, when several people later returned to the ghetto from the forest, they described how the Jews were suffering at the hands of Russian partisan thugs, and that was enough to stop anyone from leaving the ghetto. Those who came to the Bielski *otriad* later related that the "optimists"—those who were opposed to going into the forest—along with the regional commissar's most-trusted man (the engineer Altman) strutted around smugly, saying: "Well, now you see who was right. We told you that it was safer in the ghetto than in the forest. We were able to stay in our homes the whole time, and do you hear how much trouble the others suffered through, and then, at the end of it all, they came back to the ghetto?"

68 Samogon is a type of homemade Russian moonshine.

69 *L'Chaim* is a Jewish toast meaning "to life." Here, the author is implying a great drinking session.

After waiting for our people in the forest for a few weeks, the commander finally set a day for us to leave. During those weeks before our departure, we had accumulated a huge amount of food, many cows, and a large number of horses and wagons. Once again, for more than a week, we dragged ourselves through forests, fields, and rivers, but we felt very fortunate to be able to return to the Pushcha. We told ourselves that now, at least for the winter, we would be "safe" from attacks there.

When we crossed the Berezina River and entered the Pushcha region, however, we saw the aftermath of the attack, and the horrific scene of Nazi brutality unfolded before our eyes. Of the tens of villages that had been situated along the edges of the massive forest area of the Naliboki Pushcha, all that was left were piles of ash. Along the entire way, from the Berezina River to our old base, not a single house stood. The charred chimneys looked like bizarre headstones and bore witness to the fact that in those places, a hut or a village had once stood. We traveled through wheat fields filled with ripe, heavy-hanging stalks, which the peasants had not had enough time to harvest. Here and there, some had caught fire. We traveled through fields with dried-out stacks of grain sheaves. But we did not encounter a single living thing, not even a cow or a horse.

Before the war, the town of Naliboki had a large Jewish population. When the town became *Judenrein*, the local Christians "inherited" all their possessions.[70] The peasants from the town and the surrounding region lived in their houses, worked in their fields, and had no idea that they themselves would be next in line after the Nazis had finished off their Jewish neighbors. We later learned that at literally the last moment, many of the peasants managed to gather their essential household items and their livestock, and they fled into the forest to join the partisans. After the attack, the number of partisans doubled.

70 On the eve of the war, the town of Naliboki was home to approximately 350–400 people, half of whom were Jews. However, the tranquility was shattered when the Germans seized the town on June 25 or 26, 1941, unleashing a wave of abuse and violence upon the Jewish population. Subsequently in December 1941, the Jews were forcibly deported to ghettos in Rubieżewicze and Nowogródek, leading to the survival of around only twenty Jews from Naliboki by the end of the war.

The Germans destroyed more than twenty villages in the region of the Naliboki forests, and the local residents were deported to Germany to work as forced laborers. The Germans did this in order to remove the source of food, support, and connections that the locals provided to the partisans. However, they achieved precisely the opposite because by removing the owners of the sown fields, we had never had such an abundance of food.

At the time of the attack, Israel Kesler's group,[71] which consisted of fifty men and women, were not able to leave the Pushcha in time. As they were leaving, they ran into a ring of German and police units. With no other alternative, they retreated. They hid under bushes in a dense, dark corner of the forest, where they managed to survive the attack. The Germans were searching for partisans nearby, and it was a miracle that they were not discovered. Because they remained in the forest, they avoided the troubles that we had suffered during our two months of wandering.

After the attack, they took advantage of the fact that all the *otriads* had fled, and they were left as the sole owners of the region. They went to the nearby villages and took whatever they could find from the houses that had not been burned down—a large number of stray cows, horses, chickens, and much grain—and brought it back to the forest. They also took the two pots that we had abandoned at the old base. When all the separated parts of the Bielski camp reunited, Kesler's group also returned to the unified camp. Together with the goods we had brought with us, we now had a sizable supply of provisions, a herd of cows, and even 100 chickens. For the time being, that is where we set up our first base after returning to the Pushcha.

We soon reestablished the main kitchen, hung up the pots, and I took on my role as chief cook once again. At the beginning, I took great satisfaction from my hard work. We had enough of everything. We no longer had to worry about every little potato or every little piece

71 Israel Kesler was born in Naliboki. Before the war, he was a thief and even served time in prison. He had connections with local peasants and, through them, acquired weapons and gathered a group of Jewish followers around him. His relations with Tuvia Bielski were reluctant.

of meat. The people were well fed. But these good times only lasted for the duration of our time at the summer base. Later, the number of people doubled, and the situation changed entirely.

Before we knew it, autumn arrived and the rains began. The long, cold winter with its deep snow and icy winds was coming. The pressing issue now was the construction of a roof over our heads. We needed underground shelters with enough beds for our large group of people. The commander designated a crew of builders to make many large underground "huts," each of which would be large enough to accommodate several dozens of people to sleep. For this construction, the thicker trees were used. There were more than enough people who understood how to do this kind of job, and soon the work was in full swing.

A second crew consisting of several hundred people—men and women—were given the task of clearing the harvested crops that had been abandoned in the fields. The base for this crew was set up 8 kilometers from the burned-out village of Naliboki. The person chosen to lead this important work crew was named Kiveh, and he was an expert in preserving potatoes for the winter. This base became known as the potato base. As this was only meant to be a temporary base, they erected a row of small, plain huts. Plenty of tools for digging up potatoes had been found scattered near the burned-out houses. Everything would have been fine had there not been a host of problems at the potato base from the start that got in the way of gathering the necessary amount of harvested crops quickly, before the snow began.

CHAPTER SIX

LIFE IN THE BIELSKI FAMILY CAMP

We Score Treasures

The potato-base kitchen was not functioning as effectively as was needed. Not only did the workers have to carry out the necessary intensive labor but they also had to cook for themselves, which resulted in work delays. Due to these problems, the commander sent me there to organize the kitchen. When I arrived at the base and saw an enormous pile of potatoes, I yelled out enthusiastically, "My God, what a treasure!" There must have been tens of thousands of pounds of potatoes, cabbages, and beets. How much effort and risk would be needed to bring even a hundredth of that mountain of potatoes through the swampy roads of the Pushcha? And the crew continued to dig for more every day. They were literally bathing in potatoes. Oh, and what a variety of dishes the women would be able to cook up with them!

There was no equipment with which to cook in the kitchen at the potato base. There was just one small, old army pot from the time of the tsar, and it was certainly not large enough to use for such a large group of people. As soon as I arrived at the base and the people saw me in the flesh sitting in the wagon, they were overjoyed to see me. Before long, I could hear shouts coming from the huts, "Lazar has arrived!" I had really worked my way up. My reputation as a cooking expert was well known here, and I received so many invitations to reside with people in their huts that I was unable to choose one on the spot.

I eventually moved into the hut of a young man from Lida who lived alone, and I immediately got to work. When I found out about the lack of cooking equipment, I went with Kiveh, the boss of the potato base, on a horse and wagon to the burned-out town of Naliboki, where we found an enameled bathtub that had been blackened by fire and also a rusty tin pot. We brought them back to the base, and the women quickly scoured them with sand and hot water. We then hung the bathtub between two trees, using some wire. In this way, a first-class kitchen was formed, and after that, the work in the fields progressed smoothly because the laborers no longer had to cook for themselves.

While the women would dig for potatoes (*koptses*), a team of men prepared deep pits to store them. They knew how to protect the potatoes from moisture and frost as well as from the *ayin hara* (the evil eye) of strangers. These pits were well camouflaged, and they were difficult for people to find, although some unfriendly partisans discovered one of the pits and stole the few remaining potatoes from it. At this time, we also began to transfer to the winter base sheaves of dry wheat, which served as feed for the cows and horses, along with bedding material for the hideouts in the large *zemlyankas*. We had enough straw for the cows and horses to last the entire winter. (Straw was not a problem during the summer as there was no lack of field pastures.)

Who can understand the ways of Providence? With one hand God punished us, and with the other hand He blessed us. As mentioned, the Germans had this bright idea to burn the villages and drive away the owners from the sown fields, and because of this, we suddenly and unexpectedly became the owners of the entire harvest. But that wasn't all. The burned-out town of Naliboki was an enormous treasure for us, because after the fire, the ruins of the collapsed brick houses provided us with bricks, burnt tin, wire, and nails. I don't know how we could have built the winter base had it not been for the burned-out town of Naliboki.

The work of digging up potatoes was tolerable even for those women who had never done this kind of work before. Each person worked with great enthusiasm because they felt that they were doing it for themselves. As long as it was warm, it was possible to work in the field in torn shoes, even barefoot, and in a light, torn dress. But with the arrival of autumn's wet and cold weather, it became quite bitter for those who had been left with shabby, ragged clothing after the attack. We pitied these women when they returned from the fields in rags and tatters and with swollen feet.

It's important to mention that in the forest, single women could not get a decent garment on their own. Such a woman would help herself by linking up with a single man, who would somehow get something for his "wife" to wear. From such matches, there would quite often be no shortage of material for gossip.

As soon as evening fell, everyone would forget their troubles and their hard day's work in the potato field. Although the evenings were now cold, we would light fires, and everyone would sit in a circle around them. Then, the singing would begin, resounding far into the stillness of the night. We would start by singing Yiddish songs as a chorus before the solo performances began. Everybody had to render something—a song, a recitation, even a bawdy joke was an acceptable contribution.

There were two sisters in our group whose family name was Slonimczyk. They stemmed from refined, well-to-do parents from Lida. The younger one was called Mirke (Miriam),[72] and she stood out more than anyone else during these late-night concerts. I remember that she gave recitations in Hebrew, and she was acclaimed by all. Who could have known that years later, in Rome, Italy, I would meet this very same Mirke and her boyfriend, whom she was about to marry. He

72 The other sister was called Liza (her married name was Ettinger). Both sisters immigrated to Israel.

became a successful Yiddish poet, whose book of poems I typeset in Rome. Who also could have known that I would be a witness at their wedding in the Great Synagogue in Rome, and that I would participate in the celebration in honor of the publication of his first book of poems, organized by the Union of Yiddish Writers and Journalists in Rome. This was the now-famous Israeli poet Moshe Yungman.[73]

No one was in a hurry to go to sleep in the cold huts, so we would sit around the fire late into the night. These evenings would put us in a better mood and helped us to forget our troubles. When it rained in the evening, this singing was the best remedy to chase away the sadness and the sorrow that each of us carried in our heart. And even though the rain ran down our collars, it did not in the least disturb the singing that came forth from the huts. The short days and the long nights stretched out in this way.

One night, such a deep snow fell that we were barely able to crawl out of our huts. After that, we could no longer go out to the fields to dig potatoes. So within a few days, the potato base was liquidated, and we all moved to the winter base. Many events occurred while I was at the potato base and remain in my memory and, of course, among them were also some provocative incidents. After all, one can surely imagine that in such a large group of men and women, among whom there was no "guardian" of morality, there was no shortage of spicy stories.

Our Participation in the Overall Battle

The winter base was situated several kilometers from the summer base. A "street" cut through the thick forest, and there were rows of large "houses" on both sides, half buried in the ground and with roofs covered in bark that had been stripped from the trees to prevent the rain from penetrating. On top of each one was a thick layer of earth that was covered with branches to hide our *zemlyankas* from the enemy's airplanes.

73 Moshe Yungman (1922–1982) was a Yiddish poet. Born in Chodorów, Galicia (now Ukraine), he immigrated to *Eretz Israel* in 1947.

Even after the attack, we had no respite from the Germans. Their airplanes flew daily over the forests, lurking above the partisans. They would fly very low, but they rarely detected a base beneath the thick trees. As soon as we heard the roar of their engines, we would hide beneath the thick layer of branches, and the airplanes would see nothing but forest and more forest. In fact, on the very day of our move to the winter base, German airplanes suddenly flew over and detected the kitchen from which smoke was billowing. They began to shoot at the kitchen with machine guns. The people who were there quickly fled, and no one was harmed. The only casualties were two cooking pots that had been punctured by the bullets.

After everyone had settled into the large communal huts at the winter base, the commander, Tuvia Bielski, began to reorganize the *otriad*. From the time when Viktor Panchenkov had taken a large number of our best fighters along with their weapons for his *otriad*, the Bielski *otriad* was unable to participate in the battle against the enemy. But when we returned to the Pushcha with weapons that we had acquired in the region, and after we had found Kesler's group in which almost everyone had a weapon, the commander consulted with his staff and decided to renew the partisan battle against the German garrisons.

Armed groups were organized, one of which was designated to carry out diversionary and sabotage actions. Leibush Feldman, who later immigrated to Canada, was appointed commander of this diversionary group, which consisted of twenty people. Despite all his requests, Bielski rarely received any of the weapons that were distributed by General Platon's central headquarters to all the *otriads*, weapons that were coming from Soviet Russia and were being dropped by parachute. However, as it is said, "where there's a will, there's a way," and Bielski had already found a way to get the brand-new automatic weapons directly from the Soviet pilots who often landed their airplanes on the provisional airfield near our base. Before long, explosive materials and general weapons were no longer in short supply—not even in the Bielski *otriad*—and the commander was able to find a way to arm his partisans.

At the same time, Bielski made sure that those who were unarmed would also be able to contribute to the battle against the murderers of their brothers and sisters. He took upon himself a project that no other *otriad* commander in the Pushcha had ever even dreamed of doing. He set up workshops for the purpose of producing the most needed items for our *otriad* as well as for other partisan *otriads* in the Pushcha. There was no shortage of people in our group who were skilled in all sorts of trades and could run these workshops. One might think that this was a nice utopian dream. We did not have even the most rudimentary tools with which to begin. But at the time, Bielski just said that we would get everything we needed by hook or by crook. And, indeed, that is what happened.

It didn't take long before our people brought sewing machines for the tailors and furriers and all sorts of other necessary equipment for the various planned workshops. On orders from the commander, our partisans recovered this equipment from the peasants in the surrounding peasant villages who had actually stolen this Jewish property at the time of the mass murders of the Jews in those places.

The carpenters, who were busy with construction work, erected a building that was 40 meters long and 10 meters wide to house the first group of workshops. Men and women were employed there as tailors, seamstresses, shoemakers, carpenters, leather cutters, harness makers, hatmakers, and watchmakers. Separate *zemlyankas* were constructed for a weapon-repair workshop, a blacksmith, and a locksmith.

Around this time, approximately 300 additional people joined our group: fifty men and women who had fled on the way to the train as the Nazis were liquidating the Lida ghetto; a second group of 150 men who had fled from the camp in Nowogródek; and the third group of approximately 100 men who had fled from the Kołdyczewo camp near Baranowicze.[74] There were also 250 Jewish men confined in the Nowogródek camp, none of whom had any hope of remaining alive there so they attempted to escape through an underground tunnel that

74 Kołdyczewo was a farm located about 18 kilometers from Baranowicze. The Nazis established a camp there in the summer of 1942 and brought over Jews from different places, including Baranowicze, Nowogródek, and Zdzięcioł (Dzyatlava). In March 1944, the prisoners organized an escape from the camp. Many arrived at the Bielski camp, but dozens were killed during the escape.

they had dug at night over a long period of time. During this escape attempt, however, 100 of these men were captured.[75]

Among the newcomers were several good craftsmen. The *otriad* had suddenly acquired quite a few skilled tradesmen who, with their specialized knowledge, were very useful in the workshops and in other activities. There were several skilled leather workers in the group from Kołdyczewo. When they saw the hides of the slaughtered cows being buried in the ground, they approached the commander with a plan. If he could provide them with lime and tools, they would set up a leather shop. The commander saw to it that they got everything they needed, and it didn't take long before the leather shop began production. How much toil and effort the leather workers had to put forth until they finally saw their first completed piece of soft leather! And the shoemakers turned out several pairs of boots for members of staff. They did not have enough time to make hard leather because the Soviets sped up their offensive, and we were liberated.

The Bread Problem Is Solved

When work began on the winter base, it was decided that the first priority would be to build a *zemlyanka* to house a bakery and thus solve the bread shortage problem once and for all. In no time, the carpenters had built a large underground house. One of our group was a Jew who was an oven builder. The Russian word for this was *gantchar*, which we accepted as a Yiddish word. He had golden hands, and he built the

75 In the summer of 1943, the Jews of Nowogródek established an escape committee led by Berl Yoselewicz. Other members of the committee included former serviceman Jozef Jarmowski, electrician Rakowski, and several other Jews. They resolved to construct a tunnel. On September 26, 1943, the majority of the inmates successfully escaped through the tunnel, which measured approximately 200 meters (656 feet) in length, 70 centimeters (2.3 feet) in width, and 70 centimeters (2.3 feet) in height. Around 170–200 of them were able to reach the forests and join the Bielski brothers' partisan camp, while the remaining escapees were either shot during their escape attempt or were apprehended by the Germans. Berl Yoselewicz, the technical planner of the underground tunnel, was murdered by the Germans.

oven. Then, the carpenters fashioned the paddles, the kneading troughs, and all the other necessary implements. We now had a bakery like we once had at home.

With the completion of the bakery, there was still a major problem to deal with: the lack of flour. We had a certain amount of corn and wheat, and getting more corn was not a major concern as we could travel to the more distant villages on the other side of the Niemen River and take as much corn as we needed from the peasants. However, the bigger problem was grinding the corn and the wheat. The Germans had burned all the mills in the area around the Pushcha, and even if there was a mill still standing somewhere far off, it was under German control. Nevertheless, there were several times when our people managed to use that mill to grind flour. Each time, however, was fraught with great danger, and it was very difficult to drag themselves back and forth across the swampy roads. We were left with just one alternative: to build our own mill.

Almost all the village peasants had their own hand mills. Back in our old hometowns, these hand mills were used to produce buckwheat grains, which the housewives would then use to bake buckwheat bread for *Shabbos*. In no time at all, our men had dragged over several large stones, and the carpenters and locksmiths set to work. Before long, we had our own mill. We soon found a Jew who had been a miller back home and knew this trade very well, so he was put in charge of the mill. Initially, several people were employed there to turn the wheel by hand all day long, so the mill could continue to grind. Later, however, several people out on a food gathering mission found an attachment used for horses and dragged it back to the base. The workers attached it to the mill, and all day long, a couple of horses moved it round. That is when the mill went into full swing and also ground enough grain for the main kitchen.

One oven could hold eighty loaves of bread, each one weighing 1 kilogram. The bakery operated around the clock without interruption. Each loaf of bread was divided among four people per day. For some this was barely enough, but everyone was extremely happy. The bread problem was solved, but no one could forget—not even for a moment—the time when they desperately longed for a morsel of bread. Nor could anyone forget the six-day hunger we experienced during the attack. So, some of the bread was sliced and dried in the oven and made into crackers, and each person kept a small packet of these crackers in their *zemlyanka* in case of another attack. We also cooked cholent[76] in this oven. We not only did this for *Shabbos* but also sometimes on ordinary weekdays. After all, there were plenty of potatoes, so some of the women would put a tin of potatoes into the oven after the bread had been taken out, and we treated ourselves to a bit of cholent while reminiscing about the cholents of yesteryear.

The bakery also served another purpose. Once a week, during the cold winter evenings, lectures and presentations on a variety of topics were given in the bakery, and the audience would leave feeling refreshed after such an evening. The lecturer was Dr. Shmuel Amarant,[77] who had been the director of the Tarbut Hebrew Teachers' Seminary in Vilna before the destruction. He had come to the *otriad* with his wife Tamar after the liquidation of the Lida ghetto as part of the group of fifty people who had escaped and saved themselves.

The people yearned to hear an encouraging word and were desperate for information about the war front. Later, central headquarters had printing facilities, and they would print news bulletins

76 Cholent is a traditional Jewish stew. Its basic ingredients are meat, potatoes, beans, and barley. It is simmered overnight and usually eaten for lunch on the Jewish Sabbath. Over the centuries, the concept of cholent developed to conform to Jewish laws prohibiting cooking on the Sabbath. The pot is brought to a boil on Friday before the Sabbath begins and is kept on a *blech* (a metal sheet placed over a stovetop) or a hotplate until the following day.

77 Dr. Shmuel Amarant studied history at the University of Lwów (Lviv, Lvov), and at the age of twenty-three, he was awarded a doctorate. He continued his studies in pedagogy and psychology and became the director of the Tarbut Hebrew Teachers Seminary in Vilna. During the German occupation of Vilna in 1941, he was imprisoned together with his wife Tamar in the ghetto. After a short time there, he ran away and managed to get to the Lida ghetto. During the liquidation of the Lida ghetto, he hid and later managed to get out through a tunnel dug under the ghetto fence along with three other people. He managed to reach the forests together with his wife, and they both joined the Bielski partisans. He immigrated to *Eretz Israel* in 1946.

and newspapers, so we were more or less informed of the war's progress. Once in a while, an old edition of the Russian newspaper *Pravda* or *Izvestia* would find its way to headquarters. Dr. Amarant would gather some information together and, with his intuition and a little imagination, put together a presentation, thereby creating a little optimism and hope in our hearts. The people were delighted with his presentations and were thankful for the beloved Dr. Amarant, whom everybody honored and respected.

Dr. Amarant also performed another important function in the camp. Each day, he would collect testimony from different people about the Nazi atrocities in their towns. The commander saw to it that he had the necessary writing material and provided him with a separate hut for this purpose. He gathered valuable material, which unfortunately fell into the hands of the Soviet secret police who arrested Dr. Amarant and his wife Tamar after the war, when they attempted to steal across the Russian border with the *Bricha* movement.[78] Miraculously, they were able to reach *Eretz Israel*, but the written testimonies were lost.

There were two highly skilled locksmiths who worked in the weapons workshops. They were such talented specialists that when they repaired a weapon—quite often using primitive tools—they made certain modifications to a rifle or a machine gun, the results of which were so precise that it elicited astonishment from the senior authorities. They assembled rifles from rusty parts that had been found somewhere, and more sorely needed rifles were therefore added to our arsenal.

The carpenters performed extremely important work. For them, there was no shortage of material in the forest. They used a long, broad saw to cut panels from the trees. Our men brought them all sorts of tools: large and small planes, chisels, hammers, and so on. And what couldn't these carpenters manufacture from the wood? When they made a rifle butt, the lock fit so precisely that it was often hard to tell that the rifle

78 The *Bricha* (the Hebrew word for escape), also known as the *Bricha* movement, was an organized underground effort to facilitate the escape of Jewish Holocaust survivors from post-World War II Europe to Mandatory Palestine in contravention of the White Paper of 1939. Its activities ceased upon the declaration of Israel's independence and the nullification of the White Paper.

had not been manufactured in a factory. The carpenters made hundreds of such rifle butts not only for our *otriad* but also for other *otriads*. In addition to this, they produced wooden sandals that were used as substitutes for shoes, which were in very short supply, as well as tall, large vats that were used in the leather factory to soak the hides in lime. The carpenters also made two large tubs for the bathhouse, which was a major attraction in the forest and evoked great wonder from those in other *otriads* who often came to visit the Bielski *otriad*.

The tailors had plenty of work. Was there anyone who didn't need their services? People had come out of the attack in tatters, so the tailors had taken it upon themselves to patch people's clothing as best as they could or to recondition them when possible. Every once in a while, our partisans would find clothes that had been stolen from the Jews by the peasants. They would bring the clothing back to the *otriad*, and the tailors would make something out of them. In this way, we slowly patched ourselves back together. But in truth, it was not easy to get access to the tailors as they were inundated with work. After all, we were a very large group—almost like an entire small town. In addition, the tailors had to handle the work brought to them from other *otriads*, so a person had to wait months before it was their turn. But how could one complain about this?

It was even more difficult to get access to the shoemakers because footwear wore out more quickly than clothes. Shoes were constantly getting soaked either in the deep snow or when the snow melted, or they got ruined in the mud. So, the footwear would fall apart. Naturally, those who were sent out on various missions were given priority to have their shoes or boots repaired, which was more than just as they could not go out with torn boots. In the meantime, those who remained at the base had to wait many weeks for the shoemakers to repair their shoes. There was no shortage of complaints about this, although I didn't understand how one could complain.

The *otriad* also had approximately fifty horses and wagons. We had to have the necessary harness gear for the horses, which was something that we could previously get from a peasant but not any longer. The harness makers began to manufacture these items—horse collars, saddles, and so on—both for our use and for other *otriads*.

One day, as I stood stirring the soup in the pot, I suddenly heard the banging of hammers on an anvil. I asked the men sawing wood about the noise. "Didn't you know that we have a forge?" they answered. I was very interested to see how we suddenly had a forge and, indeed, not far from the kitchen stood a real forge with all the necessary equipment: an anvil, large and small hammers, and, of course, bellows. The blacksmiths had plenty of work. It would have been a headache had we not had a smithy as the wagons were constantly breaking down because of the terrible roads! And how would the horses be able to take even a single step when the frosts arrived and the roads became slippery?

The hatmakers—two brothers from Nowogródek—were very popular throughout the entire Pushcha, and partisans from every *otriad* would come to them. The dream of every partisan that winter was to have a Cossack hat. A partisan in a *kubanka*[79] did, indeed, look like a storybook hero. The two brothers along with the eldest brother's two daughters worked overtime, and they still couldn't keep up with all the orders they received. They used to joke that if the numbers of customers back home had been as plentiful as they were in the forest, every house in Nowogródek would have belonged to them!

The two watchmakers were especially fortunate because they were the only ones in the entire Pushcha who had tools—although just a few—which they had apparently brought with them from the ghetto. The Russian partisans would travel tens of kilometers on foot in order to have a watch repaired. In truth, one could get along in the forest without a watch, just as one managed without many other things. But one of the greatest pleasures for a Russian partisan was to have a pocket watch. That was really a big deal.

Another of the most popular people in the *otriad* was the seamstress Chana. There was not a single person in the camp who did not admire this refined, diligent woman who, I believe, worked harder than any of the other women in the workshops—sewing a shirt for this person, a *rubashka*[80] for another. I remember how grateful I was to

79 A *kubanka* is a high fur hat made of sheepskin and usually worn by Cossacks. It is also known as a *papakha*.

80 A *rubashka* is a kind of Russian peasant shirt.

her when she sewed a shirt for me from thick peasant linen, which the peasants would use to make sacks and that I had obtained from the senior staff. This shirt actually chafed my skin because it was so rough, like a straw mat. It took me a few days until I got used to the discomfort, but this was a minor issue compared to the pleasure I got from wearing a shirt that was not torn.

Sometime later, when the Soviet airplanes were dropping parachutes loaded with weapons, the Russian *otriads* brought these parachutes to the Bielski workshops. There was no limit to what the tailors could do with these parachutes. From the sacks, they made pants and jackets, and from the silk, they made underwear and *rubashkas*. Such a parachute was truly a treasure in the forest. On one occasion, the Bielski *otriad* received a parachute from central headquarters, which was used to clothe the most deserving partisans. I remember that several women used the parachute cords to knit sweaters. In the spring, the young women got great pleasure from wearing these sweaters while hundreds of others envied them.

A Sausage Factory, a Bathhouse, and a Hospital

The second most important venture after the bakery was the sausage factory. Among us there were knowledgeable sausage-makers, and one time, they made some sausages for us to try. They turned out so well that a plan was launched to set up a sausage factory. The commander ordered large meat machines to be brought in, and people were assigned to grind the meat by hand. Shortly after, a special oven was set up for smoking the sausages and other types of meat.

The sausage factory very quickly began distribution, and it became famous throughout the entire Pushcha. The Russian *otriads* would bring their cows to the Bielski *otriad*, and we would produce sausages for them. That was when our camp achieved great prosperity. The leftover bones went to the main kitchen as well as any remains of the cow. The sausage factory brought many benefits, although not for everyone. Only those who were sent out on battle missions or those who stood watch at their posts far from the base for days and nights would receive sausages. I remember that on May 1, however, everyone received some pieces of sausage. That was a real treat for us.[81]

It was rare that someone had a bar of soap left over from the ghetto. If one actually did have such an item, he was extremely careful not to overuse it—even with one extra rub. Instead, sand was used to clean hands, but what was one to do about washing a shirt? A solution was even found for this. We would scrape some ash from the bottom of the kitchen pot and boil it with the shirt in a pail, creating a substance like lye.[82] One can only imagine the color of the shirt after this, but no one cared—as long as the lice didn't bite.

But suddenly, our situation improved when among the Jews from the town of Balbicheva, there was someone who knew how to make soap.[83] He approached the commander and said that if he had milk, he could make soap for everyone. He was given a small container that was found lying around somewhere, and he set up a "soap factory." There was plenty of milk available from our cows, but I have no idea how he managed to get all the other components needed for making soap. The only thing I saw was that he drew tar from the trees, so the soap he made came out black. But who cared? As long as it produced suds. I remember that I wanted to say the *sheheheyanu* blessing over my first piece of soap.

As long as it was warm outside, washing oneself was not a problem. People would heat up a pail of water, take it deeper into the forest, and wash there. The situation got worse when winter came. We were no longer able to wash outside, and it was too cramped to do so in the *zemlyankas*. The women were in a very delicate situation. We all lived together and slept in the same narrow space, so the unfortunate women had to carry a pail of water outside and wash in the wintry cold. However, despite the fact that we all took care of our own personal hygiene, a typhus epidemic broke out due to the crowded conditions in the *zemlyankas*. So, the burning issue was the need for a bathhouse.

81 May 1 is International Workers' Day, something that was widely celebrated in the Soviet Union.

82 The mixture of ash and water created a substance like lye, which is used in making soap.

83 This person was Sioma Pupko.

A special brigade set to work, and behold, soon a large structure was erected at the furthest edge of the base where a source of water was available. In addition, two wells were dug nearby. The carpenters and the locksmiths installed all the necessary fixtures. First fiddle, so to speak, was again played by the *gantchar*.[84] He built a real oven that supplied hot water and—most importantly—steam for a separate steam room. Benches were installed by the carpenters, just like in the steam baths back home. From the burned-out town of Naliboki, our men dragged back pipes and faucets, and there emerged a bathhouse like the ones we had in our hometowns.

Near the oven, a small, low room was built that served as a disinfection facility. It was very hot inside this room, and while people were washing, they would hang up their clothes and underwear in this room to get rid of any lice. In this way, the disinfection process helped to end the typhus epidemic. Those who returned filthy and covered in lice from a mission, who had been wandering around on the road for weeks, were the people who experienced the most pleasure from this bathhouse. They truly felt as if they were in paradise. For them, the bath was literally a salvation when they clambered onto the uppermost bench and let the hot steam warm their frozen limbs. The bath was in use all day long, and special bath attendants ensured that there was never a shortage of hot water. Every *zemlyanka* was assigned a specified day on which to bathe.

The Bielski *otriad*'s steam bath quickly earned a reputation among every Russian *otriad* in the Pushcha and also generated enthusiasm at the staff headquarters. General Platon once visited the camp and was amazed by this accomplishment, praising the commander and the people who were responsible for building the steam bath. As the camp cook, I had the privilege of using the bath every day, and as soon as I had finished handing out breakfast, I took my place on one of the benches. Who needed anything more pleasurable?

During this same period, the hospital issue was also solved. Those with typhus had to be quickly removed from the *zemlyankas* so as not to infect others. A large *zemlyanka* was thus set up to serve as a

84 This *gantchar* is the same oven builder who had built the bakery.

hospital, but it filled up very quickly. Soon, there was not enough room to hold all the sick people, so a second hospital was built in a different location outside the base for those with contagious diseases. Shortly after the first typhus epidemic had ended, a typhoid fever epidemic broke out. The infected patients were transferred to the hospital outside the base, where they were taken care of by separate medical personnel who had no contact whatsoever with the base. They remained there until the epidemic had passed. Near the hospital, the *gantchar* also built a separate oven that was used to disinfect the clothing of the sick.

The only medicine we had against disease was aspirin or a headache powder (*kogucik*), and quite often, these were also not available. Much later, Soviet airplanes would drop parachutes loaded with medicines, and sometimes we would receive small amounts from central headquarters. But this had as much impact as if we had received no medicine at all. The most remarkable thing is that during all these epidemics, just one young man died from typhoid fever. Yes, there were other fatalities at the last base, but during the time of the two epidemics, I remember only one death.[85]

In addition to the hospital, we also had an outpatient facility staffed by a doctor and a nurse. When rashes appeared on our hands, the doctor would concoct an ointment of sulfur and tar paper to rub on the hands and the body, thus protecting us from another epidemic. Interestingly, we rarely caught a cold while in the forest despite the fact that we had broken shoes and no warm clothing. The last winter happened to be very severe with bitter frost and deep snow up to the knees that lasted all winter, yet nobody had caught a cold.

There was also a dentist—a Russian Jewish woman—who worked in the outpatient facility. I don't remember exactly from where or how she came to the Bielski *otriad*, but she was there with a daughter and a grown granddaughter. She only had a few instruments at her disposal, so she had limited ability to help those suffering from toothache. All she could do was extract the tooth, but even this was a huge relief. And was there anyone who did not have problems with their teeth?

85 See Tec, *Defiance*, pp. 245–246.

Women in the Camp

While we are on the topic of medicinal aid in our camp, it is worth mentioning another matter connected to this subject: abortions. In the forest, there were no controversies with regard to this issue. When a woman became pregnant and presented herself to the doctor, he immediately performed an abortion. One should not be surprised about this. There were many young couples in our *otriad* that had been formed both before the war and right there in the forest. Naturally, no one made any assumptions about making it out of the forest alive. We were constantly expecting more attacks, so there could be no talk of having children.

There was only one instance when a woman gave birth to a child. When she first realized that she was pregnant, it was already too late to have an abortion, and so a little girl was born in the forest. And where did this happen? In my *zemlyanka*, of course, right opposite the area where I slept! It happened in the middle of the night, and the doctor had to deliver the baby by candlelight. The entire *zemlyanka* was turned upside down, but what could be done? The child was raised in the forest, and when the weather turned warm, she developed beautifully. That is why Chaim, the person who milked the cows, coined a new name for our *zemlyanka*: Creator of Children. After the liberation, this married couple were among the stream of refugees heading for Italy, where they became part of a community of former partisans. Their family name was Abramovicz, and he was the supervisor of the food warehouse in the *otriad*.

The issue of abortions was a hot topic of discussion during the long winter nights in the *zemlyankas*. However, there was one tragic incident that occurred involving a middle-aged woman. She died following an abortion, and there was talk that it had been her own fault. I remember another case that also ended very tragically. After an incident that caused trouble in the camp, a young couple was forced to abandon their newborn infant. Who could bear to witness the anguish of these unfortunate parents?

When the partisan movement began, young Jewish women were generally not accepted into Russian combat *otriads*. The commanders were of the opinion that most of the women were not suitable for partisan warfare. But they later realized that this was a mistake. Today, we know about female Jewish heroines who, with weapons in their hands, participated in the battles against the Nazi beasts and made important contributions in various areas of the partisan campaign. But at that time, it was extremely difficult for Jewish women to join a Russian combat *otriad*, so they found a place in the family camps.

Tuvia Bielski's partisan camp was a unique amalgamation—part family camp and part combat *otriad*. Every Jewish woman, regardless of her age, was both accepted and on an equal footing under the protection of the Bielski *otriad*. The number of women at our last base in the Pushcha exceeded 400. A mere 2 kilometers from our base was another large Jewish family camp with 700 people, the majority of whom were women. Their commander was Shalom Zorin, a Jew from Minsk who had brought escapees from the Minsk ghetto to his family camp.[86]

As mentioned earlier, for a single Jewish girl without family or friends, conditions in the forest were very difficult. If a lone man was just about able to manage his personal problems there, for a lone woman it was twice as hard. It became clear that a lone woman needed a man to take care of her, so the single women or girls would try to link up with a man. In the forest, there was no need for neither an engagement nor a wedding ceremony. A couple would quickly reach an understanding, and right away they would go and live together in

86 Shalom (Simon) Zorin (1902–1974) was born in Minsk and was a carpenter. Following the Nazi invasion, he was transferred to the Minsk ghetto along with the rest of the city's Jews. He worked as a forced laborer in a camp where Soviet prisoners also worked, and he met an officer named Semyon Ganzenko there. They became friends and decided to escape from the camp together. At the end of 1941, the two fled to the forests in the Staro Selo area, about 30 kilometers southwest of Minsk. He joined the ranks of the partisans, and in 1943, he founded Unit 106, which contained noncombatant Jews and totaled around 800 people. His unit was divided into two parts: a fighting company and the family camp. Toward the end of the war, Zorin seriously injured his leg in a battle. Most of the Jews from Zorin's unit were saved. He died in Israel in 1974.

Shalom Zorin.
Photo Collection, YVA, 503/7181.

the same *zemlyanka*. We all slept in the large communal *zemlyankas* during the winter, and the "newly baked" couples did not feel comfortable sleeping together in their "nest" with neighbors on either side. But as soon as the first spring breezes appeared and the snow began to melt, several of the couples got together and built huts for themselves, and that is where they spent their "honeymoon," without witnesses. Now really, was it so necessary to indulge their desires by building a hut just for themselves?

Similar to the way it was in the Vilna ghetto, single women in the forest sought to link up with a man with a prestigious "pedigree." In the ghetto, a chimney sweep might be considered a better catch than a doctor, whereas men who owned a rifle had the highest standing here. Such a man made sure to provide his wife with a nice dress and a good pair of shoes. Also, from time to time, when he returned from a food-gathering mission, he brought something better to eat. One can imagine the anomaly of a young woman or a young widow from a fine home who had linked up with a man from a totally different background. Of course, such a union did not last very long, and as soon as the girl had somewhat improved her circumstances, she reconsidered and returned to her previous situation. There were also quite a few happy unions in the forest. And, as in every partisan *otriad*, there were also exceptions in our *otriad*. In general, women in the camp were exempt from standing guard at a post with a rifle. However, quite a few women learned how to handle weapons and were given guard duties. These women managed to thrive without the protection of a "strongman" type.

Quite often during the winter months, we would suddenly start talking nostalgically and longingly about the not-so-distant past, when there was still a world, and we still had a life. Someone would set the tone by relating an amusing episode of town life or describing a comical individual, an eccentric. And what town didn't have its own clown, its own oddball? The group would become more lighthearted, and we had something to laugh about for a while. And that, in fact, was the storyteller's objective: to elicit laughter, laughter if only with tears, but nonetheless laughter, and to forget about the sad yesterdays and the uncertain tomorrows for a while.

The offering that was easiest to "sell" was a bawdy story or a racy joke. In the forest, we were by no means bothered about relating such things in the presence of women. The forest atmosphere robbed us of feeling embarrassed, and even the women felt the same. There were also women in our group who could tell such stories, but it would be a mistake to think that there were many such bold women. The majority of the 400 women in the camp preserved their past dignity and fine character traits. In this regard, the "Mir *zemlyanka*" distinguished itself. That is where all those who had come from the town of Mir—famous for its *yeshiva* and *yeshiva* leaders—gathered. It was in this *zemlyanka* where I, and others like me who were drawn there, would sit in the evenings and draw on the well of knowledge from Mir. We would also just socialize with these people who were so learned in Judaism and who had occupied such a prominent place in the communal life of their towns. Later, I would meet with some of them in my room in the liberated Vilna.

Shtetl Belsk

The winter began very early that year, and deep snow covered the forest. Some of the *zemlyankas* remained unfinished, and we had to make do with a reduced sleeping area. But soon it was clear that we had "committed a sin" by complaining about the crowded conditions, because before long, 300 more Jews arrived, and we had to find places for them to sleep. There was no other alternative but to distribute a number of the newcomers to each *zemlyanka*. In our "house," for example, there had previously been forty people, but now we were a group of around sixty.

This is what the large *zemlyankas* looked like inside. Two rows were set up using round wooden blocks, which were not even connected with nails. Some straw was placed on top of the blocks, and everyone slept on these together—men, women, and children. Between the two rows was a narrow aisle with a small stove in the center that heated the house. There wasn't even any room for a chair or a table.

All day long, the "houses" stood mostly empty. It wasn't until the evening when everyone returned from work that the entire *zemlyanka* became jam-packed from one side to the other. Not only was there no room to sit but also there often wasn't even enough room to stand. In the evening, we would visit one another and have a chat. It was lively. The children's shouts mixed with the loud conversations of the adults created such a din that one felt they could actually go deaf. For the entire evening, things were buzzing like a beehive.

The *zemlyankas* were illuminated by candles that had been set up during the day, and even after they had burned out, no one was in a hurry to go to sleep on the hard, round blocks, so the racket continued. Even when people finally lay down to sleep, the chattering continued in the dark. And if anyone started to hum a tune, a chorus of singing would begin until people became hoarse and fell asleep.

And one more thing to mention. We slept like herrings tightly packed in a can. There were advantages and disadvantages to this. Since we slept pressed up against one another, it was nice and warm. The problem, however, was that if someone's side began to hurt because they were lying on an uncomfortable part of one of the wooden blocks and they wanted to turn over, the entire row also had to turn over. So, we had plenty to laugh about. Who could make a big deal about this? It took only a moment to remind ourselves how bad things had been in the ghetto before, when all of a sudden, the conditions in the forest seemed ideal.

When the spring of 1944 arrived, feverish construction activity began anew. Groups of people who had been living together organized and built more comfortable houses for themselves, which included separate sleeping spaces, tables, benches, and so on. Such a *zemlyanka* already had the look of a real house. After experiencing an entire winter of crowded conditions and foul-smelling air, one could breathe easily after moving into one of the new houses. Within a couple of weeks, tens of these new little houses appeared and were spread throughout the length and breadth of the base, so much so that the base took on the appearance of a typical Jewish *shtetl*. And, indeed, soon the town was given the name Belsk, after the Bielskis.

In our new, little *zemlyanka*, built by eight of us for our group, each person had his own sleeping area, and we shared the table and chairs. Simply put, the small house looked like a peasant hut that Jews used to rent during the summer vacation season. I remember that this little house was a salvation for me. After a hard day of work in the kitchen, I could at least rest up at night in my little corner. In the previous crowded conditions, I was unable to indulge in such a luxury.

Regarding the children, it would not be an exaggeration to say that no other partisan camp in the Naliboki Pushcha was as rich with children as the Bielski camp. There were 110 children aged between two and twelve in our *otriad*. We guarded this treasure with great care. These children had been literally ripped from the Nazis' clutches, and they were brought to the Bielski camp in various ways. And it was not just their parents who cherished them. The commander made a concerted effort to ensure that the children had enough to eat and that they could enjoy a normal childhood while in the forest. This was especially the case for those whose parents were no longer alive.

There were two teachers who were with the children. I remember that one of them was called Czesia Henish. These were the very same children who, not too long ago, had been imprisoned behind the barbed-wire fences of the ghettos and faced the threat of death every single day along with everyone else. Now, they had the opportunity in the forest to live a childish existence. The older children were given some elementary lessons as well as instruction in dancing, singing, recitation, and musical instruments.

In the large *zemlyanka* that housed the workshops, the carpenters built a stage, and the *zemlyanka* was transformed into a theater. We also had talented musicians among us, so we appropriated several musical instruments—a fiddle, a mandolin, and a guitar—from the local peasants and brought them to the camp. And so, an orchestra—or a trio—was created.

The teachers prepared a program with the children, which was performed before the entire *otriad*. Their first performance turned out to be quite impressive and, as I remember, it made an extraordinary impression on everyone. Prior to the show, Tuvia Bielski spoke, but he kept choking up and had to stop several times. The audience was also unable to contain their emotions at such a moment, as they were reminded of their own slaughtered children who had been cut down by the Nazi murderers. I remember how the tears flowed down the faces of all who were there. It took many long minutes until everyone regained their composure and the performance could begin.

In those few hours, the children brought great pleasure to everyone there with their singing, recitations, music, and dancing. They sang Yiddish and Russian songs, and as the audience listened, they were able to forget for a moment that they were in a forest surrounded by Nazis. It felt as if it was a school holiday during normal times. When the performance ended, a nagging sense of fear for these children crept into my heart, and I prayed to God that at least this small group of little ones should survive and emerge from the forest alive.

Later, a *zemlyanka* was built for the children to use as a clubhouse. They would gather there and the teachers would meet with them for several hours each day. The children wrote a newspaper on the walls of the clubhouse. Those who could write—in Yiddish, Polish, or Russian—expressed their thoughts in prose and poetry about their lives in both the ghetto and the forest. I remember standing in front of this newspaper on the wall for hours, reading it over and over again and pondering each line—how the children expressed their joy at no longer being in the ghetto and how good it was to be in the forest. In short, the children brought a ray of happiness into the gloomy atmosphere of concern about tomorrow and the future.

Even though our sadness weighed heavy on our hearts and souls, we still yearned for diversions and ways to try and forget. At the last winter base, a number of young boys and girls had formed an ensemble of performers. We already had a fiddle, a mandolin, and a guitar to form an orchestra. There were girls with fine voices who sang both Yiddish and Russian songs beautifully. From time to time, these musicians would perform in the large *zemlyanka* that contained the workshops. The older children also participated in these performances and displayed great talent. When the weather turned warmer, the performances were held in the open air. Everyone would sit in a circle, and the performers would be in the center.

For a while, there was a Russian in our group who had been wounded during the attack, and he was recovering in our hospital. This Russian had once been involved in professional theater, and while in the forest, he wrote a film script about partisan life. On various occasions, he read scenes from the script to me. He left us in the spring; however, a short time later, a performing ensemble of Russian partisans showed up at our base. They had an orchestra of various instruments, and they performed a song and dance show for us. The director of this ensemble was the same Russian partisan who had recovered from his wounds in our hospital. He told me then that he had organized this ensemble with the support of the central staff and that the ensemble was traveling to every *otriad*, performing shows throughout the entire Naliboki Pushcha.

The performance by the Russian Artistic Ensemble occurred several months before the Soviet army drew near to the Naliboki Forest region. It was the start of summer, so the Russians performed outside in the open air, in the center of a large circle of spectators. For a while, the members of the audience totally forgot that, at any moment, the enemy's planes could show up and start dropping bombs. But by then, we were already experienced and knew not to run away. We just had to try and get to a tree, stand under it, and see from which direction the planes were coming.

Until summer finally arrived, spring brought us the absolutely bitterest stretch of time. The melting snow created "lakes" in the camp. To cross the "street," we had to plod through deep mud and, to avoid falling into this mud, we had to jump acrobatically across stones that were scattered on the ground. The people who stayed on the base were somehow able to manage, but for those who had to travel by horse and wagon through the muddy roads, well, that was a different story. More than one group was forced to abandon their transportation in the mud and continue on foot to the base. We then had to go back with them to help pull the horse and wagon out of the deep mud. But we quickly forgot about these problems as soon as the "lakes" had disappeared, the mud had dried, and we were living in our newly built little houses.

Among our group, there were a significant number of people who did not deviate in any way from the traditional Jewish way of life that they had observed in their hometowns. They continued to follow all the laws of Halacha (Jewish law) as decreed by God. For example, there was a group of elderly Jews who prayed every day, faithfully observed *Shabbos* and the holidays, and did not eat food from the main kitchen but cooked for themselves instead. They were given as many potatoes as they wanted, and they also received goods from the food warehouse. When Passover neared, the bakers baked *matza*[87] for these observant Jews, and for the entire week of Passover, they ate only potatoes and *matza* and did not eat any food that was forbidden for this holiday. The cows were slaughtered according to the Jewish laws of ritual slaughter by the *shohet*[88] from Woronów, who had come to the Bielski camp with his wife and five daughters after escaping death in the Woronów ghetto.

In the meantime, people were in such a hurry to build their small houses that it didn't take long before "Shtetl Belsk" spread out across a couple of kilometers. No one took into account that the war front was

87 *Matza* is an unleavened flatbread that holds a significant place in Jewish tradition and is consumed during the Passover holiday.

88 A *shohet* is an individual who performs the ritual slaughter of animals in accordance with Jewish Halachic requirements.

getting closer with each passing day. That was the logic of life in the forest! Don't think about tomorrow, just live for today. Many, many incidents—some humorous and some serious—occurred in Shtetl Belsk that remain in my memory to this day.

It's important to note that when we returned to the Naliboki Pushcha after the big attack, we knew almost nothing about what was going on in the world—not even how the war was proceeding. We no longer had a radio in the *otriad*. Later, however, our reconnaissance people would return from central headquarters with a bulletin, which was distributed to all the *otriads* and contained a little bit of news about the war front. Central headquarters not only had a radio to receive messages but also a transmitting apparatus that connected them to the main headquarters of the partisans in the Soviet Union. Of course, all this radio equipment was supplied by Russian airplanes.

The partisans had built a landing strip in the vicinity of the Naliboki wilderness, and Soviet airplanes would land there from time to time, bringing various important pieces of equipment. On their return trips, they would take back any seriously sick or wounded partisans. Headquarters would receive a radio message on a designated day, saying that on such and such a night, an airplane would be landing. The message also provided instructions as to how many guide fires should be lit by the landing strip and in which direction they should be pointing.

During the winter and continuing into the spring of 1944, many Soviet airplanes landed in the Naliboki Forests as well as other areas. When the Germans became aware of this, they began flying reconnaissance planes over the forest practically day and night to prevent the Soviet airplanes from landing. Sometimes, German bombardiers would drop bombs on the provisional air base, wounding partisans who were there as part of the requirement of every *otriad* to send a large squad of armed partisans for two weeks at a time to stand guard there. And it was just when a group from our *otriad* was standing guard that the Germans bombed the airstrip. Fortunately, none of our men were harmed, and they all returned safely to the *otriad*.

A group of partisans from various fighting units who guarded the airfield in the Naliboki Forest, July 1944. Among them are partisans from the Bielski family camp.
Photo Collection, YVA, 503/7195.

Once, the Soviet airplanes delivered a printing press to central headquarters, and they began to publish newspapers in small type in Russian and White-Russian soon after. The person who organized this partisan press was Hersh Smoliar.[89] He came to our base quite often and became very friendly with Tuvia. He delivered political lectures to us several times. But most importantly, he would encourage the older children to join the Komsomol[90] during his visits and, indeed, a Komsomol unit was very quickly established in our *otriad*.

89 Hersh Smoliar (Smolar) (1905–1993) was a Jewish writer and journalist who wrote in Yiddish and was active in the communist parties of Poland and the Soviet Union. He was imprisoned in the Minsk ghetto and headed an underground military organization there. He escaped from the ghetto and joined the partisans in the Naliboki Forests, where he printed several newspapers in both Russian and Yiddish.

90 The All-Union Leninist Young Communist League, known as the Komsomol, was the political youth organization of the Communist Party in the Soviet Union.

Hersh Smoliar.
Photo Collection, YVA, 4012/94.

From time to time, these same Soviet airplanes would also bring newspapers, some of which would reach our *otriad*. Whenever I got a hold of one of these newspapers, I devoured it from the first page to the last. That is how desperate we were to read the printed word, and it was from these newspapers where we found out what was happening in Russia. Eventually, some of our men brought in a small radio apparatus—a detector with earphones—that they had found somewhere. The apparatus was kept in the commander's hut, and in the evening, we were able to pick up the latest news.

There was a small group of us who occasionally got together for a couple of hours at a time to discuss literature in a small corner of the forest. Included in this group were two *yeshiva* boys, one of whom was from the Mir Yeshiva and was very taken by this gathering. He would carry around a notebook of poems—his most secret of secrets. The other one, who had already received his rabbinical ordination, would read his sketches about forest life at these gatherings. These frequent meetings after work were a salvation for us. I remember that the Mir poet attached himself to me because I was from Vilna, which was the city of his idol Chaim Grade of whom he thought the world because of his poem *Musernikes*, and he would speak nostalgically about the group Young Vilna.[91] Almost no one in the camp knew about our small cultural circle.

91 Young Vilna was a dynamic Yiddish literary group of writers, poets, and artists who came of age—in the creative sense—in Vilna in the 1930s. Chaim Grade (1910–1982), a leading Yiddish writer born in Vilna, was a member of this group.

CHAPTER SEVEN

LAST MONTHS IN THE FOREST

The War Front Nears

We made it through the long winter, after which spring slipped in and turned everything around us green. The scent of the pine trees was in the air, and the birds greeted us with their chirping in the mornings. We no longer had to trudge through deep snow. One would think that this would have had a positive effect on our mood, as is normal when spring arrives. However, the arrival of the spring of 1944 had precisely the opposite effect on the Jews of Shtetl Belsk. A worm of anxiety began to penetrate our hearts as we could not forget—not even for a moment—the massive attack of the previous summer. When there was severe frost and deep snow, we were safe, but as each passing day brought us closer to summer, we felt that the danger of an attack was also increasing.

We soon noticed the first indications that they were planning an attack. German airplanes began to make more frequent appearances, flying over us in search of partisans. They flew so low that they almost touched the trees. Then, they dropped bombs, strafing the forest. One of these attacks resulted in a truly astonishing incident. One of the airplanes was hit by a rifle bullet. A partisan from the Voroshilov brigade,[92] using an ordinary rifle, aimed at the airplane when it flew low over him and scored a hit. The airplane crashed and was totally destroyed. We all ran to look at the demolished airplane, as if this was a miracle. This was the first time that a German airplane had been shot down by a partisan from our forest region.

The war front was coming closer and closer to us, and the partisans were now more active in executing sabotage missions. There was no lack of weapons and explosives. The Soviet airplanes were now delivering these materials in plentiful supply. The partisans endeavored to stop any transports reaching the front. If this or that sabotage group was unable to destroy a transport, another group completed the task at a different location. No matter how closely the Germans guarded the train lines, they were totally ineffective in stopping the partisans. The Germans then tried a different approach to impede the partisans' sabotage activity. They occupied all the villages and roads with large divisions of their surrogate accomplices—Ukrainians, Lithuanians, White-Russians, and Russians—to prevent the partisans from reaching the train lines while also blocking access to the villages, which were the partisans' source of food supplies.

It's true that at the beginning, we were afraid of this blockade. Several of our groups that had been sent out on food-gathering missions were forced to return empty-handed because they were unable to get through the blockade. I remember that one of the groups did, in fact, blunder into an enemy trap. Miraculously, they broke away and returned to the base unharmed. Their family and friends were already weeping and lamenting their loss.

92 The Voroshilov brigade was established in November 1942 and operated in Western Belorussia.

Our base was notified that we should be in a state of readiness. We had enough food supplies to last half a year, so we were not concerned about going hungry. Nevertheless, the daily bread ration was reduced for the time being. There were rumors circulating that the blockade was just the first phase of a much larger assault, bigger than any other offensive that had occurred in the Pushcha, and that this time, the Germans were planning to deploy regular motorized army units against us.

During this time, it was estimated that there were over 20,000 partisans in the Naliboki Forests, and even though the partisans had enough weapons, we were in no position to take on the enemy's army in open battle. Our reconnaissance men brought the news that German military divisions had begun to attack the partisans in the Lipiczanska Pushcha in the Slonim region, and it was clear to us that when the Germans were finished there, they would surround the Naliboki Forests. We sensed that the closer the war front came to us, the greater the danger would be. We told ourselves that even in the best-case scenario, even if there was no attack, we would still be crushed during the conflict between the opposing forces as the front would spread through the Naliboki Forests. We became reconciled to the thought that we had no chance of leaving the forest alive. More than anything else, we were afraid of falling into the clutches of the Nazi murderers.

Several Revolver Shots

Despite the tension caused by this newly created situation, daily life on the base continued as before. Everyone did their work, and even construction of the small huts did not stop. One day, we were all shaken up by an unusual event that took place in our camp. Since Shtetl Belsk had almost everything that a town needed, it was also necessary to have a prison. With such a large group of 1,200 people who had come together from all walks of life, there was a possibility that individuals might commit wrongdoings, and so a small *zemlyanka* was designated as a prison. The fact is, the prison was almost always empty. From time to time, someone would be held there for a day or two for some insignificant offense. But on that day, everyone was astonished by the news that had spread with lightning speed throughout the base: Kesler and his wife had been arrested.[93]

This was the same Kesler who, together with his group, had separated from everyone during the attack and had remained in the Pushcha before reuniting with the *otriad* under Tuvia Bielski's command upon our return. There were rumors of bad blood between Tuvia and Kesler. Kesler had a reputation in the camp of being a capable person. Everything that he had undertaken had been done in an orderly fashion. At the last base, Tuvia had given him the responsibility to build the hospital and to manage it afterward. However, it is also true that stories about his past were being whispered about.

The prison was located several meters from the kitchen. As I was standing by the kettle, I saw Tuvia and his brother Asael along with several other staff members passing by very quickly, heading in the direction of the prison. Several minutes later, I heard shouting and several gunshots. A little while later, everybody knew that Kesler was dead and that Asael had shot him during an extremely tense moment. Contradictory rumors circulated throughout the base. From all the talk, the final version that emerged about this incident was that Kesler and his followers had been plotting behind Tuvia's back, and news of this had reached the senior partisan command. Bielski's staff treated this as treason and did not want to let it go unpunished. I only remember that this tragic incident shocked us deeply.

Another incident involved a barber from the Lida ghetto, a refugee from Poland, by the name of Białobroda. He had set up a loathsome supplemental source of income for himself while in the ghetto. He would go to the White-Russian police and inform on Jews who were carrying food with them as they were returning to the ghetto. The police would take away this food, and the Jews would thank God that they had escaped with their lives. Afterward, Białobroda would receive a portion of the confiscated food. Those in the ghetto wished for his death. He thought no one knew about his vile deeds. One day, however, people from Lida discovered that he was on the base. In short, one fine morning, the news

93 Israel Kesler was arrested at the command of Tuvia Bielski, and Kesler's wife Rachel decided to join him in prison.

was announced that Białobroda had been killed with a bullet to the head, and everybody said, "May all our enemies end up like this."[94]

A third incident occurred on the day before we vacated the camp; however, it was considered an accident. The victim was a blacksmith by trade. He had come to the Bielski camp with his wife and some pieces of equipment just three months prior to leaving the forest. He did not want to subject himself to the general rules of discipline, and the manager of the workforce had a difficult time with him. Suddenly, everyone was jolted by the news that he was dead. I no longer recall the exact circumstances of his tragic death.

In the Russian *otriads*, very tough discipline was enforced. For a serious offense—for example, falling asleep at one's guard post—the guilty person would be shot. In the Bielski camp, however, the discipline was considerably less strict. For similar transgressions and misconduct, one got off with spending a night in prison. I guess, Jews act like Jews everywhere. That is why the Kesler episode had such a powerful impact on us. We regretted its occurrence, even though people close to the leadership said that documents existed confirming Kesler's treachery.

Before the Partisan Court

It was the middle of April. I was sitting in the commander's *zemlyanka* in the evening, listening to the radio report about the war front. Suddenly, we sprang to our feet with joyous surprise. We had just heard that the Soviet army had broken through the entire length of the front at Vitebsk,[95] and the German army was fleeing in panic. We then stayed up half the night talking in the *zemlyanka* about this important event. From that evening onward, there was a glimmer of hope that we would leave the forest alive.

94 It was assumed in the camp that Białobroda had conspired with Kesler against Tuvia Bielski. See Tec, *Defiance*, pp. 196–197.

95 During the Soviet army's offensive of 1944, Vitebsk was liberated on June 26, 1944.

The next morning, the reconnaissance men brought a bulletin listing all the areas that the Soviet army had liberated. Every day, the bulletins brought reports about more and more victories as well as the names of both the small and large liberated towns and villages of eastern White Russia. The front approached us with lightning speed, so much so that we were convinced that we no longer had to fear an attack.

The crushed German army units that were surrounded in the Vitebsk region attempted to break through the ring. Small groups of soldiers and officers set out through the endless forests, hoping to escape to the west. Apparently, they never even thought that a "true welcome" was awaiting them in the forest, courtesy of the partisans. That is when the time came for the partisans to take revenge upon the enemy and for us—Bielski's Jewish partisans—to avenge the Nazi killers for the murders of our sisters and brothers.

The German soldiers wandered around day and night through the forests, and as soon as they appeared in the Naliboki Pushcha, spies who were scattered throughout the forest immediately notified their headquarters, and units were dispatched to capture these "bigshots" very quickly. They were initially brought to headquarters to register their personal information. These fine gentlemen of the "master race" stood doubled up and contorted as if suffering from convulsions, trembling before the Jewish partisans. They would place their hands on their hearts and swear in every which way that they had, God forbid, never murdered any Jews. In fact, just the opposite—they had always loved the Jews.

One day, the Bielski partisans dragged three SS men to headquarters. They had hidden their automatic weapons in the forest after they had run out of bullets. However, when our men captured them, they were forced to reveal where they had hidden the weapons. As soon as they were brought to the base, everybody assembled near the headquarters. I was one of the lucky ones who was able to get inside. I will never forget how these three SS men were on their knees, begging for their lives because they had wives and children at home. They soon realized that they had fallen into the hands of Jews, and they swore that they were not guilty of what the Nazis—not they, God forbid—had done by murdering millions of Jews and that it was only the Führer Hitler who was guilty of that.

After the interrogation, the commander gave an order to fetch the oldest partisan in our *otriad*—Shmuel Yitzhak Pupko from Lida, a man in his late seventies—and appointed him to be the head of the partisan military court. Behold, he had lived to confront the Nazis, not as a victim but as a prosecutor. It was an extraordinary scene, watching this old, gray-haired Jew deliver the prosecutorial summation of charges with an anguished heart and shaking both his fists very close to their faces. The commander felt that the entire *otriad* should participate in carrying out the verdict and executing the sentence of the court against these murderers. One by one, the SS men were led out of the headquarters and delivered into the hands of the assembled crowd. Within a few minutes, there was no longer any sign of them. Seeing these SS men made our blood boil so much so that people who had never even harmed so much as a fly in their entire lives tore into the murderers to kill them.

From then on, the Bielski partisans threw themselves into the dangerous task of capturing these animals in human form. But they were no longer brought back to the base. Instead, they were "disposed of" on the spot. The wolves in the forest were no longer hungry. The oath that the Bielski partisans had sworn to their brothers and sisters in the ghettos—to avenge the innocent blood spilled in vain—was kept by them in an honorable way. Many times, the commander cautioned everyone to be careful so as not to lose their own lives on the very threshold of liberation. There were some Nazis who fought back right up until the final bullet. But in the end, if they became entangled in the endless forests where the partisans were roaming, they all suffered the same grim fate. Every day, we listened with great eagerness to the stories told by the men taking part in this hunt.

The Russian partisans once captured thirty Nazis who were then brought to the central headquarters. When they were searched, the partisans found photos of mass slaughters of Jews. Is there any better proof than this of the kind of people they were? It wasn't enough that they had spilled Jewish blood, but they also needed to immortalize it in pictures to delight their families. Since none of the Russian military leaders could speak German, they called for two Jews from Bielski's staff. When the two men saw these horrible pictures, it made their blood boil. Seeing the impact these photos had on them, the Russian commander said, "Take these dirty dogs and take care of them any way you want." Upon hearing these words, the two Jewish partisans Pesach Friedberg and Salomon Volkowyski[96] immediately went over to the pit where the Nazis were being held and ordered them to crawl out, line up four to a row, and march forward with their hands on their heads. They probably thought they were being taken to a prisoner-of-war camp. Two series of shots ended their despicable lives.

The Germans Attack Our Base

It was May 1, 1944. The senior staff decided to celebrate this workers' holiday in a solemn manner. No one worked that day, and reports from the front brought news of great victories by the Soviet army, so this added a festive mood to the solemnity. After breakfast, we all gathered near the headquarters for a meeting at which the commander and several staff members spoke. Their speeches recognized with honor the fallen members of our group. Following this, they read out the names of the decorated partisans who had excelled in the fighting and then expressions of thanks were given to the workers for their conscientious work in the workshops and on various projects.

Everyone received a festive meal of sausages and a double portion of bread. After lunch, the workshop building was converted into a theater. The group of performers had organized a musical performance, and this was the first time that we could enjoy ourselves in the forest for many long hours in such an exalted mood. In a word, that May 1 was a once-in-a-lifetime experience!

Interest in news of the front increased with each passing day. We could barely wait for the reconnaissance men to bring us the news bulletins from central headquarters about the swift march of the Soviet army as well as the long lists of the liberated towns. In one of the bulletins, my birthplace Vilna was listed.[97] My heart skipped a beat at

96 Pesach Friedberg was the quartermaster officer of the Bielski partisans, and Salomon Volkowyski was the head of special operations.

97 Vilna was home to approximately 57,000–60,000 Jews after the Nazi occupation.

this news. Oh, how I wanted to be there at that moment, to see the city where I had spent my entire life, both in happiness and in suffering. That night, I couldn't fall asleep, and all night long, horrible scenes of everything that had happened since I had parted from my family flashed before my eyes. In my mind, I still had a glimmer of hope that perhaps someone from my family had survived.[98]

In those last few days, larger groups of Germans were wandering through the forests trying to escape, but in their desperation, they became even more unyielding. This resulted in tough battles with them. Our leaders ordered us not to get undressed at night and to be prepared. The defense positions around the base were strengthened. In addition, with enemy airplanes above us dropping bombs and strafing us with their machine guns, we had to suspend the cooking in the main kitchen so that the smoke would not give us away. Headquarters warned us not to walk around the base too much to avoid detection. However, it was apparently preordained that we would not get away without suffering victims.

One evening, we heard the thunder of artillery very close by. It seemed that shells were exploding quite near our base. The entire sky was lit up from the rockets. It was obvious that the front was now just a few kilometers from us. Nobody slept that night. The bombardment continued throughout the night, and at dawn, it suddenly fell quiet. We concluded that the Germans had retreated and that this would be the day when we would meet the Soviet army. In the meantime, we decided to take a short nap.

Only a few thousand survived the war. Vilna was liberated from the Nazis in mid-July 1944, although fights and chaos still prevailed in the city. On July 8, the Red Army surrounded the city, and by July 13, it had been conquered. Jewish partisans contributed to the liberation of the city and returned there from the forests in the summer of 1944. About 6,000 Jews gathered in the city after its liberation, embarking on a new chapter of their lives as free people.

98 No one in Lazar's immediate family survived except for his brother Victor who had immigrated to the United States in the 1930s. His father had been killed by Poles in 1921. The rest of his family—his wife and two daughters, his mother, his brother and his three sisters along with their spouses and children—were all murdered.

A thunderous barrage of gunfire startled us out of our sleep. We jumped out of our holes and grabbed our weapons. An armed German unit had approached our base, shooting at us with automatic weapons. We opened fire on them to push them back from the base. However, it quickly became evident that we could not defeat such an enormous military force. Our only alternative was to pull back behind the base. This exchange of gunfire, however, drew the attention of neighboring *otriads*. Help arrived at just the right time, and seeing that we had received reinforcements, the Germans ran off. However, they were quickly surrounded on all sides, and not one of them survived.

Ten of our people fell in that battle. Our pain was great. These were young, heroic lads who for two years in the forest had survived many perils and had experienced every attack, and it was their fate to be felled by a German bullet at the very last moment, just before liberation. This loss had a shattering impact on us. The entire camp participated in the funeral of the ten youths who were buried with military honors. We stood by the open graves, distraught and with bowed heads, and we wept at this great loss. Among those who had been killed was Gordon,[99] a member of the staff command who had been well acquainted with General Platon even before the war. He had been the one who maintained contact with the general as the representative of our *otriad*.

At the same time as the funeral, news was racing through the base like an electric current: The vanguard of the Red Army had been seen at the edges of the forest.

99 Tanchum Gordon was born in 1905 in the town of Vasilishki near Lida, Belorussia. After his wife and daughter were murdered in Vasilishki, he managed to get to the Lida ghetto where he was an underground member, organizing groups to escape to the nearby forests. He also escaped Lida and was appointed the commissar of the Kalinin unit of the Bielski partisan *otriad*. He was one of ten or eleven partisans to fall at the hands of German retreating forces in the last days of June 1944, shortly before the liberation.

CHAPTER EIGHT

JOY AND SADNESS

A few days before the German ambush on our base, a high-ranking Soviet military official visited us. Such guests often showed up in the Soviet *otriads*, descending by parachute onto the provisional airfield not far from our base. For the first time, we saw the officers' new uniforms adorned with epaulettes, which were almost exactly the same as those of the former tsarist officers that, not too long ago, had been the symbol of the counterrevolutionaries in the Soviet Union.

The entire camp gathered in a circle and the guest made a speech. First, he thanked us for joining the ranks of the partisans and for helping the Soviet regime in defeating the German enemy. Then, he described the happy life awaiting us upon our return home, and how the Russian government would reward us appropriately for our suffering. No one was impressed by this speech, however. All of us had a clear idea of the kind of life that awaited us when we would come face-to-face with the grim destruction in our towns and cities. Later, after abandoning the base, we spoke with irony among ourselves about his promises. Where do we have a home now? None of us had any doubt that it would be a distraught life. The only good feeling that this high-ranking official left with each of us was that our liberation was at hand and, indeed, because of this, we responded to his speech with the sincerest applause.

Even before the first Red Army units appeared, we stood at the edge of our base, waiting impatiently to meet them. Multiple thunder-like echoes reverberated through the forest from our joyful shouts when we spotted the first units of the Red Army. The soldiers accepted our warm greetings with smiles. Some of them stopped for a while. They were amazed at the sight of small children. We joked around with them, telling them that these were our youngest partisans. They gave the children pieces of hard sugar, something they had never seen in the forest. For hours, we followed the marching army, running after them and engaging in short conversations with them. These were glorious moments for which we had so desperately longed and have not been forgotten to this day.

When the initial spontaneous joy had passed, the question arose: What's next? Such a question had never occurred to me while in the forest, since we had always thought that our chances of getting out of the forest alive were slim. The best-case scenario had been that we would be crushed when the front arrived. So, this sudden liberation threw us into total confusion.

Strange thoughts crept into my head. How good would it be if we could all continue to live a communal life in the *shtetl* that we had built in the forest? These people had become close to me, and the primitive life felt cherished. I even viewed the forest from a different perspective. I remember that the next day, as a free human being, I fell into a deep apathy, and I was afraid that I would have a complete breakdown. All around me, I saw faces reflecting worry and sadness rather than joy. It was evident that others—lonely people—felt as I did.

That afternoon, an order came from headquarters to be ready in the morning to leave the forest. In addition, we were told to destroy anything that could not be taken along, especially food, so that any straggling Germans would not be able to make use of it.

It was the beginning of July 1944 when we finally left the Naliboki wilderness—over 1,200 Jews, including 400 women and 110 children.

The Bielski family camp, Naliboki Forest, May 1944.
The author is in the back row, third from the left.
Photo Collection, YVA, 4613/664.

MY FATHER'S LONG JOURNEY HOME

The Soviet army liberated Vilna on July 13, 1944. Large masses of people surged onto the roads leading to Vilna, and among them was my father Lazar Engles (Engelstern). He describes his frame of mind when he first entered Vilna as:

> A tangle of anxious thoughts mixed with joyful feelings at being free after so much anguish and torture. A feeling of dread came over me when I confronted my hometown face-to-face. The streets were empty and deserted, with no living creature anywhere to be seen. I felt as if thousands of shadows from the dead were pursuing me.[1]

He remained in Vilna for nine months, until April 1945. After wandering around the city for a few weeks seeing nothing but destruction and desolation and not finding any living relatives or close friends, he realized that there was no reason to stay. He describes his thoughts at

1 Engelshtern, *Mit di vegn*, p. 21.

this time, which most likely reflect the thoughts of many other survivors in a similar situation:

> There was no choice other than to get away from here. It didn't matter where—as long as it was not here. It was clear to me that I could not make a new beginning here. But I could not think of any way to begin taking steps in this direction at a time when I did not even have a cent to my name. How would I have enough strength to begin anew when I had no will to continue. Alone, without a relative, without a redeemer, what kind of life could I expect?[2]

The apartment where he and his family had lived for ten years was now occupied by a Lithuanian family. On his first day in Vilna, he met an acquaintance who had somehow survived in a hideout inside the ghetto and had continued to live in this hideout after the ghetto liquidation. The man invited my father to stay with him and his family. Over the next several months, he met other survivors and got a job that generated enough money to cover his basic needs.

The most fortunate event that happened to my father during his time in Vilna occurred when, one day by chance, he met another survivor, a woman named Ruth, whom he had known before the war. Her husband, who had been murdered by the Nazis even before the ghetto was established, had been a close friend from his school years. She had survived two years in the ghetto and after escaping just two days before its liquidation, she found a hiding place in a barn, where she wrote the diary that I referred to in the introduction. These two survivors, who had lost everything that was meaningful in their lives, suddenly found hope, companionship, and a renewed desire to begin life anew. From then on, after their chance meeting, they would meet almost every day. Before leaving Vilna, Ruth and my father became a couple, and they got married. A year and a half later, I was born in April 1946 in a Displaced Persons camp in Italy.[3]

2 Ibid., p. 82.

3 For more information about my mother, see Leimenzon Engles, *Written in a Barn*.

Toward the end of 1944, Poland and the Soviet Union reached a repatriation agreement regarding a mutual exchange of citizens of the two countries. Former Polish citizens living in certain designated areas—one of which was Vilna—who had automatically become Soviet citizens as a result of the collapse of the Polish state, were given the right to return to Poland. My parents jumped at this opportunity to leave the Soviet Union, move to Poland, and from there continue on to the Free World. Their ultimate destination was initially *Eretz Israel*, which at that time was called Mandatory Palestine. However, that plan changed later when my mother, whose health had been debilitated during her ten months in the barn, became pregnant. She did not have the strength to make *aliya* to *Eretz Israel* on a dangerous, clandestine ship journey under *Bricha*[4] supervision. From then on, their target destination was the United States.

As soon as it was possible, they registered for repatriation, and in April 1945, they began a long, arduous, and dangerous journey through Europe that took many months. The journey took them eastward from Vilna, Lithuania, across Poland, into Czechoslovakia, continuing into Romania, and then westward into Hungary, Austria, and finally Italy. They traveled on passenger trains, freight trains, and trucks. Their last border crossing from Austria into Italy involved a hike across the Tyrolean Mountains. This was exceptionally difficult for my mother who was pregnant with me. Along the way they were assisted and guided by *Bricha* agents who also provided them with the forged documents they needed. Border crossings were particularly stressful as they nervously waited for the Soviet authorities to accept the validity of their documents.

When they arrived in Italy, they were moved from one temporary refugee camp to another until finally, toward the end of 1945, they settled in the Cinecittà Displaced Persons Camp in Rome. Because they were registered as Polish citizens and the Polish quota for immigration was very low under the strict US immigration laws, they ended up

4 As mentioned earlier, the *Bricha* was the underground effort that helped Jewish Holocaust survivors escape Europe after World War II to Mandatory Palestine. It was organized by partisans and Warsaw ghetto fighters in late 1944 and subsequently joined with a similar effort by the Hagana, the Jewish army in Mandatory Palestine.

living in the DP camp for nearly four years. During that time, my father had various jobs with the relief organization the American Jewish Joint Distribution Committee (JDC or the Joint), and he also worked at the camp's Yiddish newspaper, both as a compositor and columnist. In addition, he was active in a committee whose purpose was to help the Vilna refugees in the camp. It was also during this period, when his recent experiences were still fresh in his memory, that he began to write down notes that eventually became the basis for this book.

In 1948, the Displaced Persons Act was passed, authorizing the admission into the United States of 200,000 European displaced persons for permanent residence. In order to qualify for immigration, a refugee needed an American financial sponsor. My father's brother Victor served that role for our family. Victor had been able to get a visa to the United States in 1936. He had established a life for himself in Burlington, Vermont, where he lived with his wife and son. On November 21, 1949, the day my father arrived in the United States, the two brothers embraced for the first time in thirteen years.

In Burlington, a large furnished room in Victor's home was waiting for the three new arrivals, and it seemed like my parents had finally found a place of rest. Victor had arranged a job for my father, and he was very happy to have his brother with him in Burlington. My father's first impression of Burlington was very positive. But there was something missing that was of utmost importance to my father: "I did not find a Yiddish newspaper in my brother's house, nor a Yiddish magazine nor a Yiddish book. All the shelves were filled with English books and magazines. No Yiddish word was spoken in his home."[5]

He decided that before settling in Burlington, he would look around New York, ignoring his brother's warning that living in New York would be like living in hell. What he found in New York was:

> Not a resurrection of Vilna, but a continuation of the Vilna atmosphere. Jewish America was fully visible here in all its splendor. I was simply blinded by the large mass of Jews and Jewish institutions, with its Yiddish daily newspapers, other

5 Engelshtern, *Mit di vegn*, p. 296.

> Yiddish publications, and the Yiddish theater. New York quickly held me in its grip. I saw a possibility here to free myself from the yearning to fit in once again into a worthwhile and creative cultural life.[6]

His biggest concern was whether he could get a job in his trade as a compositor for a Yiddish newspaper or publication. When he went to the printshop of one of the Yiddish newspapers, *Der Tog Morgan Zhurnal* (The Day-Morning Journal),[7] he met two compositors whom he had known in Vilna. They assured him that they would get him into the Yiddish typesetters' union.

That is, in fact, what happened. After being accepted into the union, he got a job with *Der Tog Morgen Zhurnal*, where he worked for the next nineteen years. During the week that he spent in New York, he met other compositors and friends from Vilna and also former partisans from the Bielski camp. It became crystal clear to him that New York—and not Burlington—was the place to settle with his family. After returning to Burlington to bid an emotional goodbye to his brother, my parents and I traveled to New York, where we eventually found an apartment in Washington Heights, the neighborhood in which we resided until 1968.

During the nineteen years that he lived in New York, he became an active member of the New York Jewish community. After an initial period of acclimating to the new culture, the new language, and the new surroundings, he got involved in the many Jewish cultural activities and developed connections with various Jewish organizations that existed in New York. In one of these organizations, *Vilna Farband* (Vilna Association), which was dedicated to keeping the memory of Jewish Vilna alive, he was an active member of the board. At the newspaper he became an integral part of the typesetters' collective. As he had done

6 Ibid., p. 299.

7 In 1949, the paper was actually called *Der Tog* (The Day). In 1953, it merged with the *Der Morgen Zhurnal* (Jewish Morning Journal) and became *Der Tog Morgen Zhurnal* (The Day-Morning Journal). In 1971, to the great sorrow of my father, the paper, which was the second-largest Yiddish daily newspaper in America, ceased to publish.

in Vilna, he not only set type for the paper but also wrote many articles about the various current affairs of the time, both in the local and in the broader Jewish community.

In 1953, my mother became ill. Although she recovered at that time, her health continued to deteriorate, and on July 7, 1955, she passed away at the young age of 45. At the time of her passing, my father was writing a series of articles about his memories of the ghetto and forests in the monthly periodical *Der Amerikaner* (The American), which was published by *Der Tog Morgen Zhurnal*. The magazine was widely distributed to several countries, including Israel. One of the people in Israel who read these articles was a woman called Pnina Burshtin. She had known my father in Vilna where they had been neighbors. She had immigrated to *Eretz Israel* in the 1930s, had gotten married, and had two children—a boy and a girl. She wrote a letter to my father reintroducing herself and informing him that her husband had recently died. A correspondence began between her and my father, which led to her coming to the United States. Eventually, in July 1956, they became husband and wife.

The idea of *aliya* to Israel, which had been my parents' original intent in 1945, now returned to my father's thoughts. In fact, that idea had never departed from his thoughts:

> For the entire time that I was in America, I did not have the feeling that this was the final stop on my life's path. I always emphasized during my conversations with friends that since I had already had the honor of surviving death, it was my debt on my own part and that of my child[8] who remained after the destruction, sooner or later to make *aliya* to Israel.[9]

A few years after he married Pnina, he visited Israel and met her family. During his five-week visit, he also met many Vilna acquaintances and

8 My father would have been very pleased to know that my wife Eva and I made *aliya* to Israel in 2021 and that our entire family—children, grandchildren, and great grandchildren—all reside in Israel.

9 Engelshtern, *Mit di vegn*, p. 349.

former Bielski partisans. Knowing that in Israel there was already such a community of people with whom he had so much in common gave him the confidence that he would be able to easily integrate into Israel. Over the next few years, the plan to move to Israel upon his retirement in 1968 crystalized. The fact that I would be graduating college in 1967 and continuing my education in graduate school also facilitated their immigration plans.

Through his writings in *Der Tog Morgen Zhurnal* and his active involvement in the various Jewish cultural initiatives, my father had become a prominent member of the New York Jewish community. On April 30, 1968, the *Der Tog Morgen Zhurnal* family organized a farewell evening for him and Pnina. In his autobiography, in a chapter titled "From Dream to Reality," he wrote:

> May 24, 1968, was an unforgettable day in my life. On that day, I stepped onto the soil of *Eretz Israel* as a new immigrant. A liturgical-like and pleading prayer quietly arose from within my breast—"May this land of Israel be the last stop of my wanderings toward which I yearned when I left Vilna in 1945 with the stream of Holocaust refugees and finally arrived here after a delay of nineteen years."[10]

During the first few weeks after their arrival, a "deluge" of former partisans descended upon the couple with hearty welcome greetings to Israel. It did not take long for him to become deeply involved in the cultural activities of the Tel Aviv Jewish community. He was very involved in the building of Beit Vilna (Vilna House) in Tel Aviv. This was to be a cultural home that would represent a living monument for the destroyed "Jerusalem of Lithuania." My father felt very honored, especially as a new immigrant, to be selected as one of the nine members of the committee that was given the task of developing Beit Vilna. This became the focus of his life for the next six years, and much of his time was devoted to bringing this project to fruition. In 1974, the project was completed, and Beit Vilna became a museum and cultural

10 Ibid., p. 360.

center whose purpose was to keep alive the memory of Jewish Vilna. It is still active today, sponsoring many cultural events related to the history of Jewish Vilna. My father considered his contribution to the establishment of Beit Vilna to be one of his proudest accomplishments. He was also elected to be a member of the administration of the Israeli Vilna Association and became involved in publishing a monthly journal called *Der Vilner Pinkes* (The Vilna Register).

Lazar speaking at Beit Vilna, 1974. The Warsaw ghetto fighter Antek Zuckerman is sitting next to him (far right).

Soon after he arrived in Israel, my father began to write articles in a Yiddish newspaper that was called *Yiddisher Tzeitung* (Yiddish Newspaper). The articles reflected the perspective of a new immigrant about the various issues and problems that were current at that time in Israel. The editor of the paper found out about the series of articles he had written in the magazine *Der Amerikaner* about his Holocaust experiences. After reviewing my father's notes that were used for these articles, he agreed to print weekly chapters based on the notes. The series ran for fifty-two weeks in 1970 and 1971, titled *Fun ghetto un vald* (From Ghetto and Forest).

Yisrael Rudnitzki, one of my father's Vilna acquantances and an expert on Holocaust literature, contacted him and told him that his memories were worthy of being printed as a book. Nobody, he said, had written so broadly and in such detail about the Bielski partisan camp—how they had battled against the Nazis and how they had survived in the forest. Rudnitzki offered to edit his handwritten notes in preparation for publication. His long-held dream of publishing both his own memoirs and my mother's diary was achieved in 1972.

For many years, my father continued to write, to actively participate in Jewish cultural life, and to maintain his connections to the many Vilnaites and former partisans who lived in Israel.

Lazar's membership card for the Association of Yiddish Writers and Journalists in Israel, c. 1969.

In 1976 he published his autobiography *Mit di vegn fun der sheyres-hapleyte*. That was also the year that my stepmother Pnina passed away. In 1978, my father came for a visit to the United States and for the first time met his two grandchildren: four-year-old Michael and one-year-old Ruthy. A few years later, in 1982, when health issues had slowed him down and he was in an assisted-living facility in Israel, our family came to visit him, and he had a second chance to get to know his grandchildren before he passed away two years later, on January 27, 1984, at the age of eighty-one.

These two Jewish children—his grandchildren—who many years later are raising their own families in Israel and continue to observe the Jewish traditions, the Yiddishkeit that was so centrally important to my father, represent his victory over the Nazis who destroyed his family.

David Engles

Lazar Engles, postwar.

Lazar and his son David, the translator of this memoir, 1968.

Four generations of the Engles family at the 50th wedding anniversary celebration of Eva and David Engles, Jerusalem, Israel, 2021.